Canvas of the Hidden Heart

Canvas of the Hidden Heart

Hugo Cortés Ruiz

Mesh Studios Inc.

First Edition — 2026

ISBN: 978-1-0696851-2-4 Paperback
ISBN: 978-1-0673684-4-9 Hardcover
ISBN: 978-1-0673684-3-2 eBook

Published in Canada by Mesh Studios Inc. Toronto, Ontario, Canada.

Cover design and interior layout: Mesh Studios Inc.

Printed by Amazon KDP.

Dedication

For those who have learned that love is not a straight line, but a thread that refuses to break.

Contents

Canvas of the Hidden Heart
Title Page
Copyright
Dedication
Preface
Whispers of Innocence 1
The Spark of Us 11
Fading Footsteps 21
Equations of the Heart 31
Shattered Silence 39
Brushstrokes of Becoming 49
Worlds in Colour 57
Echoes of Home 65
Almost Seen 73
The Weight of Expectations 81
Digital Ghosts 89
When the Heart Returns 97
Threads of a Shared Canvas 105
Echoes in the Hum of the City 113
The Garden of Time 121
Threads of the Past, Fabric of the Future 129

The Language of Silence 137
The Embrace of London 143
The Unfolding Chapters 149
Epilogue 155
Acknowledgments 161
About The Author 163
Books By This Author 165

Preface

In the geography of the human heart, there are no straight lines.

We are taught to believe in trajectories. We are taught that life moves from Point A to Point B: from childhood to adulthood, from solitude to partnership, from question to answer. We are handed maps drawn by those who came before us—marked with clear highways and brightly lit intersections. Here is school. Here is work. Here is marriage. Here is the end.

But the map is not the territory.

Real life—the kind that unfolds in the quiet spaces between life's magnificent events—is a landscape of detours. It is a series of spirals, dangerous curves, and unmarked paths that vanish into the undergrowth. It is filled with dead ends that turn out to be shelters, and shortcuts that lead only to cliffs.

This is the story of two men who lost the map.

It is the story of Patrick, who sees the world as a canvas of shifting colours, where memory is a pigment that never quite dries. And it is the story of Harold, who sees the world as a blueprint of structural loads, where every emotion must be calculated carefully to prevent collapse.

They were once children who built a world together beneath a lilac bush in Ealing. They became young men who let go of each other's hands in a university laundrette, frightened by the weight of their own bond. And they grew into older men who would eventually learn that the longest road is sometimes the only way home.

This is not a story of a grand, cinematic romance. There are no airport chases, no public declarations, no duels at dawn.

Instead, it is a story about the quiet, stubborn courage of staying.

It is about the kind of love that survives in negative space: in the silence of a phone call never made, in the thread of a scarf kept in a drawer for twenty years, in the ghost of a hand resting on a shoulder.

It is a story about how we break, how we heal, and how sometimes we discover that the pieces we believed were lost have been carefully kept for us all along waiting for the moment when we are finally brave enough to claim them again.

And it begins, as all things do, with a single spark in the dark.

Chapter 1

Whispers of Innocence

Patrick Evans arrived in the world in the quiet dawn of 1973, at King Edward Memorial Hospital, greeted not by fanfares, but by the pale light that slips softly between night and morning.

From his first breath, he belonged to Elizabeth and Christopher Evans, a London couple whose love was constant and modest, a presence that never demanded attention yet never faltered. Patrick was their only child, the singular axis around which their small universe revolved.

Their home in Ealing was simple, but it breathed warmth. The bookshelves bowed under the patient weight of poetry and worn paperbacks, their spines cracked from years of rereading, as if they were old friends. Every spring, the garden responded to the season with lavender blooms, whose fragrance drifted through the open windows to settle on the furniture like a fine, sweet dust.

In a corner of the living room stood an old piano, its wood dulled by time, whose keys coaxed out melancholic melodies whenever Elizabeth played on rainy afternoons. The music lingered there as memories do soft, inevitable, tender, filling the spaces between the furniture with a heavy, comforting silence.

"Listen," Elizabeth would whisper when Patrick was barely a baby, cradling him against her side on the piano bench, letting the vibration of the strings hum against his small ribs.

She would press a key, letting the note hang suspended in the air, stopping time for a fraction of a second.

"Do you hear how the note holds?" she would ask, her voice low and reverent. "It does not want to leave."

Patrick, his eyes wide and dark, could not yet respond with words, but his body would grow still, listening, absorbing the resonance as if it were nourishment.

As he left early childhood behind, Patrick did not become the loud, stumbling toddler his parents had expected. At three years old, he was a creature of deliberate stillness. While other children his age banged pots or chased pigeons, Patrick would sit in the tall grass of the back garden, as motionless as a garden statue.

One afternoon in 1976, Christopher found him crouching near the rosebushes, his face mere centimetres from the damp earth.

"Pat?" Christopher called softly, approaching him with a red rubber ball in his hand. "Don't you want to play catch?"

Patrick did not look up. He raised a chubby finger to his lips.

"Shhh," he whispered. "The green walker is sleeping."

Christopher knelt beside him. On a low leaf, a brilliant green beetle rested motionless.

"It's just an insect, son," Christopher said, smiling.

"It's not just an insect," Patrick said, his brow furrowed in concentration, already showing that precocious seriousness that would define his life. "It's an emerald with legs. If you wake it up, it might lose its shine."

Christopher looked at his son, surprised by the strange and poetic logic. He put the ball away in his pocket.

"All right, Pat," he said, placing a hand on his son's small shoulder. "We'll let it sleep."

Those were the first lessons Patrick absorbed before even stepping foot in a classroom: that sound mattered, that gentleness was real, and that a home could be a silent agreement to protect trivial things.

By 1978, at five years old, Patrick entered the brick and ivy enclosure of St. Benedict's Primary School. His small hand disappeared into his mother's palm as they crossed the threshold, his eyes darting nervously between the polished floors that reflected the fluorescent lights and the unfamiliar faces blurring into a sea of grey uniforms.

The air smelled of industrial wax and chalk dust, a dry scent that coated the back of his throat and stifle the familiar smells of home. Somewhere down the hall, a bell rang, and the noise pierced his bones, sharp and demanding, cutting through the peace of the morning.

"You'll be fine," Elizabeth murmured, kneeling so her face was level with his.

She smoothed his bangs back, her fingers cool against his forehead, and then adjusted the stiff collar of his uniform, which felt like a cage.

"If it feels too loud, you can breathe slowly," she told him, searching for his gaze. "Like you do when we listen to the rain or watch the beetles in the garden."

Patrick nodded, remembering the stillness of the garden, though now his throat felt tight, as if he had swallowed a stone that refused to dissolve.

"Will you be here when it's over?" he asked, his voice small and fragile.

"Always," she said, and kissed his forehead, sealing the promise. "Always."

That same year, Harold Carrington began his own journey within those walls. Neither noticed the other back then. Fate, as it often does, preferred patience. Their names lived on separate lines of the register. Their lives, however, were already in orbit.

Patrick was a boy of quiet corners. During recess, while others screamed themselves hoarse in games of tag that looked more like wars, he gravitated towards solitude. He spent his time beneath the sprawling oak tree at the edge of the playground, with its gnarled and ancient roots, or lying on his back in the grass, watching the clouds drift and dissolve into nothingness.

Joy came to him in fragments: the whisper of the wind through the leaves, the way sunlight fractured into floating motes of dust across a classroom window. His imagination was vast and unregulated, a private ocean where castles floated in the sky and ancient animals spoke in riddles beneath canopies of moss and shadow.

Sometimes, Mrs. Hargreaves—his first-grade teacher—would pause beside his desk, her shadow falling over his drawings.

"Patrick Evans," she would say softly, as if weighing the shape of his name on her tongue.

She would tap a fingernail against the wood of his desk, a crisp sound that pulled him back into the room.

"Tell me. Where have you gone off to this time?"

Patrick blinked, and the classroom snapped back into focus, forcing the castles to crumble behind his eyes.

"I was... thinking," he would answer, his voice barely a murmur.

Mrs. Hargreaves would lower her voice conspiratorially, leaning in closer.

"Thinking is allowed, you know. But try to bring your pencil with you."

Patrick would smile, embarrassed but relieved, and the pencil would move once more, tracing unexplored worlds onto the paper.

Harold, by contrast, moved through the world with an innate steadiness. Even at five years old, there was something grounded about him. He shared cookies without hesitation, helped teachers carry stacks of books without being asked. His laugh rang clear and unreserved, and his smile had a way of settling the air around him, as if chaos simply decided not to persist in his presence.

At home, Harold lived amidst routines: his father Arthur's toast at half past six, his mother Margaret's careful columns of household figures. Praise arrived in measured portions, like sugar in tea. Harold learned early to be useful. Useful children were noticed.

In first grade, they were merely classmates: two boys in the same row, with interactions limited to the occasional shared glance or the awkward collaboration on a group project. Yet, slowly and imperceptibly, the currents began to shift.

The turning point arrived disguised as an ordinary lunch. Patrick had brought a battered, dog-eared book about the cosmos from home. Its pages were swollen from use, the corners softened like old fabric, and the spine was held together by clear tape peeling at the edges. Between its covers lay distant nebulas and galaxies, planets that looked like marbles dropped onto black velvet.

Harold noticed it the moment Patrick pulled it from his backpack. His own lunch—two triangles of cheese sandwich wrapped in wax paper—sat untouched for a full minute as curiosity took hold.

"Is that yours?" Harold asked, leaning closer, stepping into the small sanctuary Patrick had built around himself.

Patrick tightened his fingers on the cover, reflexively protective, shielding the universe he held.

"Yes."

Harold hesitated, then tried again, carefully, as if approaching a skittish animal that might bolt.

"What's it about?"

"Space," Patrick said, and felt foolish for stating the obvious.

Then, as if pulled by the gravity of the book itself, he opened it. The scent of old paper and ink drifted between them.

"Look. That's Saturn. It has rings."

Harold's eyes widened, reflecting the glossy image of the gas giant. It was the same look of wonder Patrick had when he watched clouds shape themselves into dragons.

"Are they real?" Harold asked, his voice hushed.

"They're... made of ice, I think," Patrick said, squinting as he read the caption, trying to decipher the secrets of the text. "And rock."

Harold leaned in until their shoulders touched, a solid, warm presence against Patrick's arm.

"It looks like it's wearing a hat."

Patrick's laugh came out unexpectedly sharp and bright, like a small bell ringing in a quiet room. Several children nearby glanced over, then returned to their shouting, dismissing the moment.

Beneath the noise, Harold's voice dropped, turning conspiratorial.

"Can I borrow it?" he asked. "After school. I'll be careful. I promise."

Patrick's stomach fluttered with an unfamiliar sensation: fear mixed with a thin, surprising pleasure. Someone wanted something of his. Someone wanted to share his world.

"All right," he said.

Then, because he couldn't help himself, excitement bubbling up, he added, "It has incredible pictures of Mars."

They spent the rest of lunch huddled together, whispering theories about alien civilizations and the terrifying pull of black holes. Harold made sound effects under his breath—whrrr, zzzsh—and Patrick corrected him with solemn authority, as if he were a true astronomer charting the stars.

"What if," Harold whispered, touching an image of the Milky Way, "there's someone in there who can see us? As if... we were the picture in their book."

Patrick stared at the page until the stars blurred slightly, dizzy from the scale of the thought.

"Then maybe," he said carefully, "we should do something worth seeing."

Harold looked at him, and something in that gaze felt like a door swinging open, letting in a fresh, bright wind.

That afternoon, fuelled by the images in the book, they embarked on their first collaborative adventure. Behind the school gymnasium, where discarded cardboard boxes were stacked like abandoned furniture, Harold dragged a large one out with a triumphant grunt.

"Spaceship," he declared, patting the side of the box.

Patrick's hands hesitated, uncertain, seeing only cardboard where Harold saw chrome and steel.

"But it needs windows."

"We'll make them."

Harold found a broken ruler and began sawing at the cardboard with the earnestness of a carpenter framing a house.

Patrick crouched down, the smell of damp paper filling his nose, and began planning aloud, his mind racing to fill the empty shell.

"We need controls. And a seat. And... and a name."

Harold paused, the ruler still in his hand.

"Name?"

Patrick nodded, feeling his cheeks grow warm.

"Ships have names."

Harold considered this, wiping a smudge of dirt from his cheek, his brow furrowed in thought. Then he smiled.

"The Star Chaser."

Patrick's eyes lit up.

"Yes. And we're going to..." He stopped, surprised by the ease of their agreement. "We're going to Mars first."

They worked until the winter light grew pale and thin, with shadows stretching long across the playground. Patrick used scraps of paper to create buttons and taped them to the inside; Harold reinforced the walls with extra cardboard. When the bell rang, signalling the end of clubs and the beginning of parent pick-ups, they climbed inside their crude creation.

It was dark inside. It smelled of sticky tape, dust, and pure imagination.

Harold clicked on a small flashlight, and the beam of light turned the cardboard into an illuminated stage, casting long, dramatic shadows.

"Captain Patrick," Harold said, his voice solemn, stripped of all irony.

Patrick swallowed and then accepted the role the way one accepts a crown.

"Captain Harold," he replied. "Prepare for liftoff."

Harold made a roaring sound, shaking the box so that the outside world vibrated and disappeared. Patrick laughed again, and for the first time, he did not feel strange for being himself. He felt... part of something.

As days turned into weeks, Patrick's afternoons often unfolded in his grandmother Eleanor's cottage, a refuge where real life seemed to pause. It was a place where ivy climbed freely and roses bloomed with a rebellious confidence. Eleanor, a former textile artist, carried a quiet strength in her posture and an understanding gaze that missed nothing. She allowed Patrick's imagination to exist without restriction: she let him arrange porcelain dolls into elaborate narratives, let him drape himself in old scarves and hats, transforming into whoever the day required.

On the mantelpiece, a row of porcelain figures stood like an audience waiting for the curtain to rise: a ballet dancer frozen mid-twirl, a gentleman in a top hat, a little girl with a painted tear on her cheek. Patrick loved them because they never demanded he explain himself. He could turn them into heroes, villains, lovers, wanderers. He could turn them into anything.

Eleanor would watch from her armchair, the rhythmic click of her knitting needles keeping time like a metronome, the wool gathering in her lap like soft clouds.

"Tell me, "She would say, peering over her glasses, her eyes bright with interest. "Who are we today?"

Patrick held up a scarf—deep green silk that felt like water in his hands—and draped it over his shoulders.

"I am a forest king," he announced, standing taller.

"And what does a forest king do?" Eleanor asked.

"He protects everyone," Patrick said, as if it were obvious. "Even those who get lost."

Eleanor would nod, as if receiving a truth. Then she would lean forward and kiss his knuckles.

"You have a beautiful soul, my darling," she would say.

Patrick felt something settle inside him: an invisible warmth that lingered even when the outside world was loud and demanding.

One summer afternoon, as the heat pressed against the cottage windows and bees buzzed lazily in the garden, Harold's hesitant voice came through the telephone.

Patrick held the receiver between his shoulder and ear, the coiled cord wrapping around his arm like a vine.

"Hello?"

"Hi," Harold said. "It's me. Harold."

Patrick's heart gave a little jolt of surprise, a bird taking flight in his chest.

"Hi."

There was a pause, filled with the faint sound of Harold's house: dishes clinking, a radio playing a tinny melody, someone calling his name. Then Harold cleared his throat.

"Can I come over and play today?" he asked, and the words sounded like something brave, a risk taken.

Patrick looked at the porcelain dancer on the mantelpiece. Fear tightened his chest: fear of laughter, of judgment, of exposure. What if Harold thought he was strange? What if the magic of the cottage dissolved under a new gaze?

He swallowed his fear.

"Yes," he said quickly, before he could change his mind. "Gran is here. She doesn't mind."

Eleanor, hearing the tone in Patrick's voice, raised her eyebrows in a silent question.

Patrick covered the mouthpiece and whispered, "Harold wants to come over."

Eleanor's smile softened into something welcoming.

"Invite him," she mouthed wordlessly, as if it were the simplest thing in the world.

An hour later, Harold arrived at the cottage door, his cheeks flushed from cycling and his hair tousled by the wind. Patrick met him on the path, hands tucked awkwardly behind his back, twisting his fingers.

"Hi," Harold said again.

Then, because he never quite knew what to do with his nerves, he offered a packet of biscuits.

"Mum said I should bring something."

Patrick took them as if they were a sacred offering.

"Thank you."

Inside, the cottage smelled of roses and old books, a scent that felt like history. Eleanor appeared from the living room, wiping her hands and arms on her apron.

"So," she said warmly, "you must be Harold. I've heard about you."

Harold straightened up, suddenly polite, smoothing his shirt.

"Hello, Mrs.... um..."

"Eleanor," she corrected gently. "And you can call me Gran if you like. Everyone does."

Harold looked at Patrick, who nodded his encouragement.

"Gran," Harold repeated, and the word sounded strangely natural in his mouth, fitting perfectly.

They stepped into the living room, where sunlight spilled through the lace curtains, painting patterns on the floor. The porcelain dolls waited on the mantelpiece. Patrick hovered near them, feeling a knot in his stomach, anticipating the inevitable mockery.

Harold's eyes swept across the figures, taking in the stillness of the room. Patrick braced himself for laughter.

But Harold stepped closer and lifted the little ballet dancer carefully, as if she were fragile in a way that mattered. He turned her in his sturdy fingers, studying the painted folds of her skirt with genuine curiosity.

"She looks like she's about to dance," Harold said, wonder softening his voice.

Patrick exhaled slowly, relieved enough to sway on his feet.

"Her name is Clara," he said quietly. "She is... she's brave."

Harold looked up, meeting Patrick's eyes.

"Brave how?"

Patrick hesitated. Then he answered honestly, because Harold's face invited honesty.

"She dances even when she's afraid."

Harold nodded, as if that made perfect sense.

"That's the best kind of brave."

For hours, they built stories together. Patrick gave each doll a name, a secret, a purpose. Harold supplied the adventure: a storm at sea, a villain in a tower, a rescue mission that required cunning rather than strength. Eleanor listened, knitting, occasionally offering tea and lemon biscuits as if she were feeding an entire kingdom.

At one point, Harold held the gentleman in the top hat and made his voice deep and dramatic.

"I am Sir Edmund the Explorer. I have crossed deserts. I have battled snakes. I have..."

Patrick interrupted, laughing.

"He hasn't battled snakes. He's afraid of snakes."

Harold's eyebrows shot upward.

"Oh, is he?"

Patrick nodded, delighted by the flaw.

"Yes. But he doesn't tell anyone."

Harold softened his voice, making Sir Edmund whisper a confession.

"I am not afraid. I am... cautious."

Patrick laughed again, and Harold joined in, their voices weaving together until even the dolls seemed brighter, bathed in the warmth of their shared invention.

Later, when Harold left, the sunlight had shifted to late-afternoon gold, stretching long shadows across the lawn. Patrick stood by the window watching him wheel his bicycle down the path, the silence of the cottage returning.

Eleanor stepped up behind Patrick and placed a hand on his shoulder.

"You were happy," she said quietly.

Patrick blinked, as if surprised by the observation.

"Was I?"

Eleanor's hand squeezed gently.

"Yes. And you were yourself."

Patrick swallowed.

"He didn't laugh."

Eleanor's eyes softened, understanding too much.

"That's because Harold sees you," she said. "And because you are worth seeing."

From then on, their friendship wove itself into the rhythm of daily life. They built blanket forts in Patrick's living room, the air inside smelling of fabric and secret breath. They raced their bicycles down the hill near the park, the wind tearing tears from their eyes, blurring the world into streaks of green and blue. They drew comics together: Patrick sketching heroes and villains while Harold wrote sharp, witty dialogue in block letters.

Their superhero duo became an obsession: Starboy and Comet, two friends who saved the world not with brute strength, but with kindness and cunning.

One afternoon, lying on the rug in Patrick's bedroom, Harold chewed on the end of a pencil. The wood of the pencil was splintered where his teeth had marked it, a sign of his concentration.

"What if," he said, "Starboy can't fly unless Comet believes he can?"

Patrick paused mid-sketch. The scratching sound of the pencil ceased.

"Why?"

Harold shrugged, uncomfortable with the truth behind the idea.

"Because... sometimes you need someone to tell you that you're not making it up."

Patrick stared at Harold, the pencil in his hand suddenly heavy with meaning.

"I'm not making it up," he said softly.

Harold held his gaze, his eyes clear and direct.

"I know," he said, simple and certain.

A rainy afternoon arrived in late autumn, the kind that turned the outside world into a blur of grey water. Patrick and Harold were sitting on Patrick's bed, their backs against the wall, listening to the rain drum against the windowpane. Elizabeth's piano music drifted up from downstairs: slow, melancholic, as if even the sound were muffled by the weather.

Patrick's chest felt tight, the way it always did when the world grew quiet enough for thoughts to rise like silt in water.

He turned to Harold, the question trembling behind his ribs.

"Do you think we'll always be friends?"

Harold blinked, surprised by the sudden seriousness. Then his expression settled into certainty.

"Of course," he said. "Always."

Patrick searched his face, as if looking for cracks in the promise.

"Even when we're older?"

Harold snorted softly.

"Especially then. When we're older, we'll have... I don't know. Jobs. Houses. We'll still meet up."

Patrick's voice dropped to a whisper.

"What if we go to different schools?"

Harold frowned, thinking hard, wrestling with the immensity of the future.

"Then we'll still meet up. We'll ride our bikes. Or take the bus. Or..."

He shrugged, frustrated by how big the world felt. Then he leaned forward and pressed his fist lightly against Patrick's shoulder, the way he did when he wanted to anchor something that was drifting away.

"You're Patrick. You're... you're a part of me."

Patrick held his breath. Warmth spread through him, fierce and terrifying.

"I am a part of you," he repeated, tasting the words as if they were new.

Harold smiled, embarrassed by his own honesty.

"Yes. So, stop worrying."

Patrick nodded, though the worry did not fade. Instead, it transformed into something fragile and sacred, a promise he felt he had to protect at all costs.

Downstairs, Elizabeth's piano shifted to a brighter chord, fighting against the gloom. The rain continued, steady as a heartbeat. And in that shared stillness, with Harold by his side and the world softened by water, Patrick felt the seed of something unspoken settling between them: not merely friendship, but a deeper recognition, a bond that did not yet have a name.

For the first time, he understood the feeling of being safe; not because the world was harmless, but because someone had chosen to stay.

And outside, the oak tree in the garden shuddered in the wind, its leaves whispering like turning pages, as if time itself were already beginning to write what would come next.

∞∞∞

Chapter 11

The Spark of Us

The summer of 1984 did not arrive; it invaded. It slid over Ealing like a held breath finally released, pressing down upon the slate roofs and tended gardens with a dense, golden weight that refused to lift.

School did not end with the cinematic drama Patrick had expected—no bells ringing to stunned silence, no papers thrown joyously into the air to fall like snow—but with a collective shrug. A final scrape of chairs against linoleum, the dusty smell of chalk settling one last time in the sunbeams, and then the doors swung open. Suddenly, the days stretched before them unmeasured, bright, and privately thrilling.

The air thickened, becoming something palpable. By July, the heat was a physical burden on the shoulders, a warm hand pressing down. The tar between the paving stones on Culvert Avenue softened until it shone like obsidian, viscous and treacherous, ready to trap the heel print of a trainer forever. The lilacs lingered past their season, dropping their heavy heads over the garden fences, stubbornly perfuming the breeze as if unwilling to let go of spring.

Patrick met Harold on the corner of Culvert Avenue every morning. It was a ritual that required no verbal confirmation, a silent pact woven into the fabric of their friendship. They did not own watches. In 1984, time was not a digital imposition, but a fluid negotiation with the sun. Patrick measured the morning by the slant of the shadows against the brick flank of the post office, or by the distant, metallic chime of the ice cream van two streets away, before it surrendered to a tired, mechanical hum.

That Tuesday, the heat was already rising in shimmering waves from the tarmac, distorting the air like a mirage. Patrick leaned against the wall, kicking a loose piece of grit, the sound scraping against the quiet of the neighbourhood. He watched a blackbird wrestle with a worm on Mrs. Gable's lawn, a brutal and silent tug-of-war, a small violence amidst the suburban peace.

When Harold finally rounded the corner, he walked with that distinct, purposeful stride that was already beginning to define him: shoulders square, head high, moving as if navigating a grid only he could see.

"You're late," Harold said, stopping three feet away.

He crossed his arms, his posture stiff. His t-shirt, a faded red, had a small hole near the collar, a flaw that somehow made him seem more real, more accessible.

Patrick squinted into the sun, shielding himself with a flat hand against the glare.

"No. I'm early... for the rest of the day."

Harold frowned, the expression wrinkling the bridge of his nose, trying to parse the statement.

"That makes no sense."

"It should."

Patrick pushed off the wall, dusting the brick grit from his palms.

"It means I'm stealing time from the afternoon."

Harold considered this, processing the logic as if it were an equation that didn't quite balance. Then, a small, reluctant smile tugged at the corner of his mouth, cracking his usual seriousness.

"You say the oddest things sometimes, Pat."

"Come on."

They walked side by side, their trainers scuffing the pavement in a syncopated rhythm: scuff, step, scuff, step. Unburdened by backpacks, their spines felt straighter, their shoulders lighter, as if a great invisible yoke had been lifted from them, leaving them weightless.

Patrick noticed everything that morning. The world seemed to have turned up the contrast. He smelled the sharp, green scent of freshly cut grass fermenting in the heat; he heard the low, sleepy drone of bees dismantling the rhododendrons with methodical precision; he caught the faint crackle of radio static drifting through open windows: news about miners' strikes and pop songs about broken hearts, all blending into the soundtrack of suburbia. Summer felt less like a season and more like a place, a distinct country they had immigrated to, and Patrick wanted to memorize its geography inside his chest.

They reached the park, a sprawling ribbon of green bordering the railway line. The stream that cut through the centre was low, the water crawling lazily over smooth stones, reflecting the canopy of leaves and the sky in broken, shifting fragments of blue and green.

A storm the previous week had brought down an ancient horse chestnut tree. It lay across the water like a fallen giant, a monument to gravity. Its roots were a tangled mass of earth and torn fibres, reaching into the air like grasping fingers, while its trunk formed a precarious bridge to the far bank.

Harold stopped. He inspected the trunk with a critical eye, looking where the bark had splintered, revealing the pale wood beneath. He stepped onto it, testing the integrity of the wood with his full weight. The tree groaned, a low, woody complaint that vibrated through the still air.

"Do you think it'll hold?" Harold asked, glancing back over his shoulder.

Patrick looked down at the water. It wasn't deep, but the bottom was thick with silt and sharp stones, hiding secrets.

"Probably."

"'Probably' isn't very reassuring. It's like saying 'who knows'."

"It's an adventure, Harold. Go on, go."

Harold went, but he went the way Harold did: methodically. He held his arms out for balance, knees bent, eyes fixed on his destination. He moved like a tightrope walker, calculating the coefficient of friction of his trainers against the dry bark.

Halfway across, the trunk narrowed. The water below gurgled, darker here, running faster. Harold froze. He wobbled, just once, his arms windmilling slightly before he corrected his centre of gravity. He stopped and turned back to look at Patrick, who was still on the bank.

Patrick expected a challenge. He expected Harold to shout, "I dare you," or "Bet you can't do it." That was the currency of boys their age: competition, the constant proving of worth through risk.

Instead, Harold held out his hand.

The gesture was so simple, so devoid of bravado, that it hung in the air like a question. I am here. Are you coming?

For a moment, Patrick hesitated. He looked at the hand: the square nails, the slightly dirty knuckles, the lifeline etched into the palm. It wasn't just a hand; it was an anchor in a shifting world.

Patrick stepped onto the trunk. The wood felt alive beneath his feet, vibrating with the current of the stream below. He took three quick, uncertain steps, the air rushing past his ears, and then reached out.

He took Harold's hand.

Their palms sealed: warm, damp, and absolute.

The shock travelled up Patrick's arm and settled in his throat. He felt the pulse in Harold's wrist against his own fingertips, fast and steady, an impatient pendulum. Thump-thump. Thump-thump. The world shrank to the rough bark beneath his feet and the terrifying, wonderful necessity of holding on.

They moved together. When Harold took a step, Patrick took a step. When Harold leaned left to counter the curve of the trunk, Patrick leaned right to support him. They were a single organism negotiating a hostile environment, balancing each other perfectly.

When they reached the far bank, neither spoke immediately. They jumped down into the tall grass, their legs vibrating with adrenaline. They let go of each other's hands slowly, fingers trailing, as if releasing something incredibly fragile that might break if dropped too quickly.

Harold cleared his throat, turning to look at the reed beds lining the water. He was searching for words to neutralize the intensity of the moment, to bring them back to safe ground.

"The reeds," Harold said, pointing. "They look like quills."

Patrick blinked, still feeling the ghost of Harold's grip on his palm. "What?"

"Like writing quills. Green ones. Dipped in ink."

Harold pointed to where the dark water stained the bottom of the stalks.

"As if they're waiting for someone to write with them."

Patrick looked. He really looked. And there it was: the poetic precision Harold kept hidden beneath his layers of logic. It was a secret language only Patrick was allowed to hear, a glimpse into the machinery of Harold's soul.

Patrick laughed, a sharp, bright sound, startling a heron from the shallows. The bird launched itself into the air, wings beating against the heavy atmosphere, long legs trailing like landing gear.

"Did you see that?" Patrick whispered, watching the grey shape dissolve into the trees.

Harold nodded, his eyes wide.

"Yes. As if it was waiting for us."

The afternoons adopted the rhythm of a sacred ritual. By unspoken agreement, they established a sanctuary within a dense thicket of lilacs behind the old church graveyard. It was a forgotten corner of the borough, overgrown and wild, where civilization had retreated.

They fortified the space. Harold directed the construction, of course. They wove discarded carrier bags—Waitrose green and Tesco stripes—through the low branches to create walls. When the sun hit them, the plastic filtered the light, turning the interior into a cathedral of mauve and gold, a stained-glass window made of rubbish.

Inside, the air was still and secret. Motes of dust floated in the sunbeams like fireworks in slow motion.

"This is headquarters," Harold announced one afternoon, wiping sweat from his forehead with the back of his arm.

Patrick lay on his stomach on the flattened cardboard they had dragged in for a floor, his chin resting in his hands.

"Headquarters for what?"

Harold looked around, checking the structural integrity of a woven branch.

"For us," he said simply.

The declaration hung there. For us. Not for the gang, not for the school, not for the world. Just them.

They hoarded treasures there, burying them in a rusty biscuit tin they had found. A chipped marble containing a galaxy of blue swirls. Three foreign coins—francs and pesetas—that smelled of copper and travel. A heavy torch wrapped in red cellophane that, when switched on, turned their faces into strange, alien landscapes.

Patrick watched Harold organize these items. He didn't just throw them into the tin. He placed them. The marble here. The coins stacked there. Harold organized even imaginary spaces, as if chaos were a personal affront to him. Patrick loved that about him. He loved that Harold believed the world could be ordered, even if Patrick knew it was mostly a mess.

One scorching afternoon, Patrick arrived clutching a prize: a half-used, high-quality pad of graph paper he had nicked from his father's study. The lines were pale blue, precise, unforgiving.

"For drawing?" Harold asked, eyeing the grid.

"For planning," Patrick corrected solemnly.

They lay side by side, shoulders touching, knees occasionally brushing as they shifted positions. The smell of the paper—clean, chemical, sharp—mixed with the scent of dry earth and lilacs.

They sketched lunar cities. Or rather, they built them together.

Patrick drew the vision: towering glass domes, walkways that floated by magnetism, gardens that grew upside down. He drew the feeling of the place.

Harold took the pencil to add the reality. He drew the water filtration systems. He sketched the structural supports for the walkways. He calculated the transport routes.

"You have to have a way to get the rubbish out," Harold muttered, shading in a pipe system with intense concentration.

"It's a lunar city, Harold. Do we really need sewers?"

"People are still people, Patrick. Even on the moon. Things have to work."

Patrick watched Harold's hand move. The pencil was an extension of his mind: deliberate, careful.

"You're always thinking about how things work," Patrick said softly.

Harold shrugged, not looking up.

"Someone has to."

"And it doesn't bother you? Being the one who worries about the plumbing while I draw the floating gardens?"

Harold stopped. He looked at the drawing: the chaotic, beautiful swirl of Patrick's imagination anchored by the sturdy, logical lines of his own. He looked at Patrick, his eyes dark and unreadable in the filtered gold light.

"Not if you make them pretty," Harold said.

The words settled in Patrick's chest, expanding there. Safety before identity. Harold would keep the walls standing so Patrick could paint them.

The evenings belonged to the Broadway cinema. It was the only place to escape the heat. The air conditioning was overenthusiastic, smelling of stale popcorn and damp carpet, a stark contrast to the boiling tarmac outside.

They sneaked into films that were just within their age limit, or sometimes slightly beyond, buying tickets from a bored teenager who didn't care to check their birth years. They sat in the velvet darkness, pockets full of pear drops that stuck together in the heat, sharing a giant Coca-Cola with two straws.

Their fingers brushed more than once around the cold, sweating cardboard sleeve of the drink. Each time, a strange, electric jolt shot up Patrick's arm, dissipating in his shoulder. He never pulled his hand away first. Neither did Harold.

They went to see The NeverEnding Story. The cinema was packed, a sea of held breaths.

When the scene in the Swamps of Sadness began—when Artax, the white horse, started to sink into the black mud—Patrick felt a rising panic that had nothing to do with the film. The despair on the screen, the idea of giving up, of letting sadness swallow you whole, felt terribly real.

He watched the horse stop fighting. He watched the boy, Atreyu, screaming, pleading.

Patrick felt his eyes burn. His throat constricted, tight and painful. He hated crying. He hated the vulnerability of it. He blinked hard, staring at the exit sign, trying to anchor himself in the physical world.

A hand nudged his arm.

Without taking his eyes off the screen, Harold passed him a string of red liquorice.

Patrick took it. His fingers brushed Harold's. Harold did not pull away. He kept his fingers anchored to the armrest, only millimetres from Patrick's.

"Thank you," Patrick whispered, his voice cracking.

"It's silly," Harold murmured. His voice was thick, too.

"It isn't," Patrick whispered back. "It's just sad. He's losing his friend."

Harold nodded. In the flickering light of the screen, Patrick saw a glint of tears in Harold's eyes, quickly blinked away.

"Yeah..."

They sat there in the dark, the liquorice untasted, bound by the shared tragedy of a fictional horse, the silence between them louder than the film.

July bled into August, and the heat became ruthless. The tarmac shimmered with mirages. The bees sounded sleepy, drunk on pollen, stumbling through the air. They bought frozen Jubblies from the corner shop—triangles of solid ice that tasted vaguely of orange chemicals—and pressed them to the backs of their necks until their skin went numb and red.

They ended up under the apple tree in Harold's back garden. The fruit was still hard, small green bullets hidden among the leaves. A plastic paddling pool sat abandoned on the lawn, its surface filmed with yellow pollen and drowned insects.

Harold sat on the edge of the grass, flicking the water with his fingers. The drops jumped, catching the sun like diamonds before falling back.

Patrick watched the water ripple. The air was too still, heavy with humidity.

"Let's go to Ealing Common."

Harold looked up, squinting against the glare.

"Why? It's ages away."

"There's wind up there. It's higher."

They walked instead of cycling. It was too hot to pedal. Their shirts clung to their damp skin, translucent in places. By the time they reached Ealing Common, sweat was tracing slow, ticklish paths down the backs of Patrick's knees.

They headed for the cluster of silver birches near the centre, where the shade pooled thick and cool. It was a relief, like stepping into chillydop water.

Harold stopped, prodding something half-buried in the leaf litter with the toe of his shoe.

It was a single roller skate. Pink leather cracked and peeling. The laces had rotted away, leaving only rust-stained eyelets.

"Lost property," Harold declared, crouching down to inspect the axle.

Patrick knelt beside him. He threaded a long blade of grass through the wheel and spun it. It turned with a reluctant, high-pitched squeak. Eeee-errr. Eeee-errr.

For no reason at all—it was the heat, or the exhaustion, or the absurdity of a single pink roller skate in the middle of a wood—they collapsed.

Laughter bubbled up from Patrick's stomach, uncontrollable and jagged. Harold started to giggle, a rare, hiccupping sound. They fell back onto the grass, ribs aching, gasping for air, while dragonflies darted away from the noise.

The laughter died down slowly, replaced by the heavy, rhythmic sound of their breathing.

Beneath the birches, they lay on their backs. The leaves trembled overhead, thousands of tiny green flags scattering coins of light across their faces.

Patrick turned his head.

Harold was already looking at him.

The distance between them was negligible. Patrick could see the flecks of gold in Harold's brown eyes. He could see the pulse jumping in the hollow of Harold's throat.

A drop of sweat slipped from Harold's temple, tracing a path down his cheekbone, heading for his jawline.

Without thinking—bypassing the part of his brain that worried about rules or consequences—Patrick reached out. He wiped the sweat away with his thumb.

Harold hitched his breath. A sharp intake of air.

He didn't move. He didn't pull away. He let Patrick's hand linger on his face for a second, two seconds, an eternity.

The space between them tightened, charged with a sudden, terrifying gravity. It loosened again only when Patrick slowly withdrew his hand.

"I wish we could stay here," Harold whispered. The words were barely exhaled, fragile as glass. "No school. No nothing."

Patrick's voice felt trapped in his chest.

"We could build a treehouse. Live up there, in the branches."

Harold smiled, a small, private thing.

"You'd paint it. Bright yellow."

"And you'd make sure it doesn't fall down."

"Yeah. I would."

They lay there, the clouds drifting like ships across an ocean sky. Patrick felt something new settling inside him: an awareness both thrilling and terrifying. The world had tilted silently on its axis. Friendship, which had been a sturdy, predictable house, had suddenly grown a new room, a door he hadn't noticed before. He wasn't sure if he was allowed to open it.

As the summer deepened, sliding towards the inevitable return of September, they found excuses to linger.

The ends of days became drawn-out negotiations. On street corners. At the rusty iron gates of the park. At the edges of driveways where gravel met pavement.

"Tomorrow," Harold would say, scuffing his shoe on the ground.

"Tomorrow," Patrick would echo, unwilling to turn away first.

One night, Patrick stood in his bedroom, pressing his face against the cool glass of the window. The sun had set, leaving a purple stain like a bruise on the horizon. He searched the twilight for the flicker of Harold's red t-shirt, disappearing down the street.

He couldn't see it. Harold was gone for the night.

But he felt the day settling inside him like a second heart, steady and insistent. It beat a new rhythm. We are here. We are here.

It whispered something he didn't yet have the vocabulary for, a language of graph paper and fountain pens, of holding hands over deep water, of sweat wiped from a cheek in the silence of the woods. It was the terrifying, beautiful realization that he was no longer the sole author of his own life.

Harold was co-writing it now.

Chapter III

Fading Footsteps

September of 1984 did not arrive; it imposed itself. It came sideways, dragged in by a wind that stripped the air of its warmth and plastered damp, rotting leaves to the soles of Patrick's stiff new leather shoes.

St. Benedict's Secondary School was a fortress of red brick and harsh echoes, a monolithic structure that loomed over the suburb like a sentence. It smelled of pungent floor wax, damp wool, and the heavy, pervasive scent of cabbage from the institutional kitchen, which seemed to have been boiling since the war.

The transition from the small, safe world of primary school was violent. Here, the corridors were rivers of noise, a chaotic flow of bodies slamming against lockers, shouting insults that sounded like greetings and greetings that sounded like threats. The air vibrated with a testosterone-fuelled energy that made Patrick's skin prickle.

The first bell on Monday rang: a sharp, mechanical shriek that made Patrick flinch. The new timetable, printed on pink paper that already felt damp in his sweating hand, was the map of his exile.

Mr. Hargreaves, their form tutor, was a man who seemed to have been eroded by thirty years of teaching boys. He wore a tweed jacket that smelled of chalk dust and resignation. He organized the seating plan with the careless indifference of a god who had lost interest in his creation.

"Sit down," Hargreaves barked, pointing a chalk-covered finger toward the rows of wooden desks.

He pinned Patrick to a desk in the front row, next to Lucy Fenton. Lucy was all sharp angles and skepticism, smelling faintly of strawberry lip balm and eraser dust. She arranged her pens with military precision, creating a barricade between them.

"And you," Hargreaves gestured over Patrick's head, dismissing him. "Back there. Next to Pike."

Harold walked past Patrick. He did not look down. He walked to the third row and slipped into the chair beside Darren Pike. Pike was a creature of kinetic energy and noise, a boy whose laugh cracked like splitting wood and who already knew how to swear with conviction.

Patrick sat rigid. He could feel the space opening behind him. Between his desk and Harold's stretched an aisle no wider than a standard ruler, thirty centimetres of scuffed linoleum marked by generations of shoes. But in the geography of St. Benedict's, it was an ocean. It was deep enough to drown in.

The divergence began slowly, then happened all at once. It was a separation of species, inevitable and cruel.

At break times, the playground turned into a territorial battlefield. The football pitch was the high ground, ruled by the boys who grew fast and shouted loud. Harold, to Patrick's silent devastation, learned the dialect of the pitch immediately. He learned the short, aggressive nouns; he adopted the verbs that ended in bruises.

Patrick watched from the periphery. He retreated to the library, a sanctuary of dust and silence presided over by Mrs. Gable, who guarded the books as if they were her own children. Patrick would sit in a corner, pretending to research the Aztecs for History, but mostly he drew.

He drew feathered headdresses. He drew the sharp profiles of warriors. But the warriors always had Harold's nose, the precise curve of his jaw. He drew eyes with eyelashes that were suspiciously long, dark strokes of charcoal that smudged if he touched them, leaving grey thumbprints on the page like shadows.

One morning, Harold arrived late to the classroom, flushed and breathless. There was a smear of mud on his cheek and a grass stain on the knee of his grey trousers shaped vaguely like the British Isles.

He sat heavily behind Patrick. The heat radiating from him was palpable: the smell of sweat, damp earth, and the metallic taste of adrenaline. It was a scent that belonged to a world Patrick could not enter.

Patrick wanted to turn around. He wanted to reach out and trace the shape of the stain. He wanted to ask if the dirt on the pitch still smelled the way the dirt in their lilac hideout smelled: rich and secret.

He turned halfway in his seat, the wood creaking.

"Harold?"

Harold looked up, his eyes distracted, still tracking the flight of an imaginary ball. Pike leaned over, whispering something that made Harold let out a dry laugh: a harsh, strange sound, devoid of the gentle humour Patrick knew.

Lucy Fenton kicked the leg of Patrick's chair. Hard.

"Don't," she whispered, without looking up from her reading book.

She tossed her red fringe out of her eyes with a sharp jerk of her head.

"He's busy trying to fit in with them."

Patrick looked at Harold, who was now punching Pike on the shoulder in a display of camaraderie that looked painful. The moment folded in on itself into a sharp square. Patrick tucked it away behind his heart, where the edges could not cut him.

They still met at the corner of Culvert Avenue every dawn. The ritual survived because their mothers expected it, and because breaking it would require a conversation neither of them knew how to start.

But the silence had changed. It was not the comfortable, companionable silence of the summer. It was a silence crowded with unspoken things, a thick fog that separated them even as they walked shoulder to shoulder.

"Here," Harold said one Tuesday, reaching a hand into his jacket pocket.

He pulled out an oatmeal raisin cookie, wrapped in cling film that crinkled loudly in the quiet street.

"Mum made them," Harold said.

Patrick took it. The warmth of Harold's pocket still clung to the plastic.

"Thank you."

He bit into it as they walked. It was good, but it tasted different. It tasted blander, generic. It tasted safer, as if Margaret Carrington had baked them for a stranger, or for a crowd, rather than for the two boys who used to build lunar cities.

"Did you do the math?" Harold asked, staring straight ahead at the pavement.

"Yes. The fractions were tricky."

"You just have to find the common denominator," Harold said automatically, reciting the rule.

"I know."

They walked side by side, their backpacks thumping with a dull thump-thump rhythm. They spoke only to confirm logistics: assembly times, gym kit requirements, the weather. When they reached the heavy double doors of the school, they stopped.

"See you," Harold said.

"See you," Patrick echoed.

Inside the doors, their shadows continued together for a fraction of a second longer than their bodies, before tearing apart like wet paper. Harold turned left toward the lockers where Pike and the others waited. Patrick turned right, toward the library.

October brought a fog that tasted of coal smoke and orange peel. It clung to the wool of their jackets, dampening the fabric until it smelled like wet sheep, and curled the pages of their exercise books.

The school organized a bonfire on the back field to celebrate Guy Fawkes Night. It was a mandatory event, a desperate attempt by the Parent-Teacher Association to foster "community spirit" in a place that thrived on division.

The air was freezing. Parents stood in huddled circles, clutching polystyrene cups of lukewarm soup, while the boys ran wild in the dark, their shouts swallowed by the night.

Patrick stood near the art block, leaning against the rough brick wall. He was with the "Art Crowd," a loose affiliation of outcasts. There was Carole, drowning in a duffel coat three sizes too big, and Steven, a boy with nervous hands who hugged his sketchbook like armour against the world.

"It's bloody freezing," Carole complained, her breath forming plumes in the air like dragon smoke. "And the fireworks are rubbish."

She was right. The display was a dismal affair. The rockets hissed upward with high hopes but popped in disappointing bursts, like sighs of resignation against the vast black sky.

Across the fire, the popular crowd had gathered. The flames roared, consuming the wooden crates, casting long, dancing shadows that stretched and warped across the grass like restless spirits.

Patrick saw him.

Harold was standing close to the heat; his face flashing in and out of the strobe light of a Roman candle. He was laughing, his head thrown back, his mouth open. The firelight carved gold into his cheekbones and turned his eyes into dark, unreadable wells. He looked beautiful, and he looked utterly unreachable. Darren Pike had his arm thrown over Harold's shoulders, claiming him.

Patrick felt a physical ache in the centre of his chest, a tightness so severe he almost rubbed his sternum to massage the pain away.

Lucy Fenton appeared at his side, muffled in a scarf that covered half her face. She followed Patrick's gaze across the fire.

"He's not worth it, Pat." Her voice was low, half-lost to the crackle of burning crates and the fizzing fweee of a Catherine wheel.

Patrick flinched.

"I don't know what you're talking about."

"Course you do."

She nudged him with her elbow, gently but firmly.

"He's already decided who he wants to be. And it isn't with you."

Patrick pretended not to hear her. He reached into his pocket and pulled out a sparkler he had been saving. He did not light it. He simply gripped the cold metal wire. He clenched his hand into a fist, tighter and tighter, until the wire bent against his palm, leaving a pale, angry crease that would linger for days.

At home, the telephone rang less.

The silence in the evenings was heavy. Harold's mother had taken a second job auditing council taxes to make ends meet. She left notes instead of meals. Harold started talking about "tea" as something you assembled from a packet—instant noodles, a sandwich—rather than a ceremony of buttery toast soldiers and stories.

Patrick would sit in the hallway, staring at the rotary dial telephone, willing it to ring. He listened for the ghosts of the old rituals: Harold's father shouting crossword clues in the background, the hysterical aria of their whistling kettle.

But when he called, usually to ask about homework, the background was completely silent. All Patrick heard was the neutral quiet of a house conserving the warmth it could no longer afford to lose.

"Page 42?" Harold would ask, his voice tinny through the receiver.

"Yes. Questions one through five."

"Right. Thanks."

"Harold?"

"Yeah?"

"...Nothing. Just calling."

The line would click and die, severing the connection.

Even so, fragments survived. Small pieces of the old world that had not been entirely eroded by the tide of the new.

One Tuesday in late November, Patrick was sent to the office to collect the register cards. The corridor was empty; the classrooms sealed behind closed doors. The only sound was the squeak of his own shoes on the polished vinyl.

As he passed the music room, he heard it.

The piano. A battered upright that sat in a corner, usually ignored, draped with a dust sheet.

Someone was playing Greensleeves.

It was not a confident rendition. It was hesitant, searching. The notes stumbled, then found their footing. Da-da-da... da-da-da-da...

Patrick stopped. He knew that touch. He knew the specific weight of those fingers; the careful way they approached the keys.

He stepped up to the small window in the door and peered through the wire-reinforced glass.

Harold was inside, alone. He was sitting on the bench; his blazer discarded on the floor like a shed skin. His head was bowed over the keys, his shoulders rising and falling with the phrasing of the melody, as if he were breathing through the instrument.

He looked smaller in that room. The armour of the football pitch was gone. He looked like the boy who had built a headquarters out of lilac branches. He looked like the boy who worried about water filtration systems on the moon.

Patrick stepped back, unseen. He pressed his spine against the cold wall of the corridor, closing his eyes. He tried to graft the rhythm of the piano onto his own heartbeat. Thump-thump. Da-da-da.

He stood there for the entire song. When the final chord faded, hanging in the dusty air, Patrick pushed off from the wall. He walked away quickly, his shoes squeaking like wet glass, carrying the secret of the music with him.

He knew Harold had heard him. He knew Harold knew he was there. But neither of them turned. Neither of them spoke. The moment remained like a secret chord between them, vibrating just below the audible range, proving that the connection was not dead, only buried.

December stripped the trees bare, leaving them like charcoal scribbles against a slate-grey sky.

The school began rehearsals for the nativity play. It was a tradition no one enjoyed but everyone endured. Mr. Till, the drama teacher, assigned roles with a tired predictability.

Harold was cast as Joseph: stoic, secondary, required to stand still and look supportive.

Patrick was assigned to the set design crew. He was tasked with painting the backdrop: a Bethlehem night sky on a massive sheet of canvas.

They worked in the same hall but at different hours. Harold rehearsed in the afternoons; Patrick painted in the evenings.

Only once did their schedules overlap. Harold arrived early for a dress rehearsal, and Patrick had stayed late to finish the stars.

The hall was draughty, smelling of old curtains and drying paint. Patrick was perched on a stepladder, applying dots of white and silver onto the deep ultramarine blue he had mixed. He was using cheap glitter that flaked off like frost every time the canvas moved.

"It's very blue," a voice said from below.

Patrick froze. He looked down.

Harold stood at the foot of the ladder, wearing his Joseph costume: a striped tea towel draping his head and a brown tunic that looked like a sack.

"It's night," Patrick said, gripping his paintbrush.

"I know."

Harold tilted his head, studying the canvas.

"You made the stars too bright."

Patrick looked at his work. The stars were aggressive, swirling explosions of light against the dark.

"They're meant to guide wise men, Harold. They have to be bright."

Harold raised a hand as if to touch the wet paint, then thought better of it. He dropped his hand to his side.

"Maybe they'll guide someone else," he murmured. His voice was low, wistful.

"Like whom?"

Harold looked at Patrick then. Really looked at him. The mask slipped. For a second, he was just Harold.

"Like anyone who is lost."

The words hung suspended in the air like incense.

Then the caretaker's keys jingled in the corridor outside. The spell shattered. Harold stepped back, the mask of Joseph sliding back into place.

"Better finish," Harold said, turning away. "Mr. Till will go mad if the paint is wet."

The last day of term brought a fog so thick it muffled the bell. The world outside the windows was a white wall.

They emptied their lockers into plastic carrier bags. The building exhaled a final breath of chalk dust, sweat, and anticipation.

Patrick was clearing out his desk when he found it. Wedged behind a stack of forgotten exercise books was a folded paper aeroplane.

It was made of graph paper.

Patrick's heart hammered against his ribs. He unfolded it carefully, smoothing out the creases.

Inside, in Harold's cramped, precise handwriting—an architect's handwriting—was a single sentence:

Meet me at the oak tree when the moon rises.

No signature. No date. But Patrick knew.

He refolded the paper along the sharp creases. He slipped it into his jacket pocket, next to a chipped enamel football badge Harold had given him weeks earlier: a peace offering that Patrick had never worn but had never discarded.

That evening, the house was stifling. Patrick told his mother he felt like going for a walk to clear his head. She looked up from her sewing, surprised. It was freezing cold outside. But she saw something in his face—a restlessness, a need—and she nodded. Even parents recognize the gravity of first secrets.

The moon, when it finally rose above the fog, was thin as a clipped fingernail, sharp and cold.

Frost silvered the grass in the park. Every blade looked enamelled, fragile enough to snap. Patrick's breath came in small ghosts that hurried ahead of him into the dark.

The oak tree stood where it always had, beside the stream. But tonight, stripped of its leaves, it seemed to have grown. Its trunk was black iron; its branches were a maze of cracked sky.

Harold was already there.

He stepped out from behind the trunk. He wore a dark hoodie pulled low; his hands shoved deep into his pockets. His eyes gleamed in the moonlight like wet pebbles.

For a long moment, neither moved. The distance between them was five feet, but it felt like the aisle in the classroom.

Then, Harold pulled a hand from his pocket. He produced two sparklers, leftovers from the failed bonfire night.

He held one out.

Patrick took it. The wire was freezing against his skin.

Harold struck a match against the rough bark of the oak. The flare was blinding. He touched the flame to the tips of the sparklers.

Hiss.

The world shrank to a crown of white fire hissing between them. The light was harsh, bright as magnesium, illuminating the frost on Harold's eyelashes and the tension in his jaw.

They did not speak. Instead, they moved their hands.

They printed their names in afterimages against the darkness. Large, looping signatures that lingered on the retina for seconds before fading.

H-A-R-O-L-D. P-A-T-R-I-C-K.

Patrick traced a giant "S" for space. Then, emboldened by the dark, he traced a heart. He did it quickly, pretending it was accidental, a slip of the wrist.

Harold saw it. Or he didn't. His expression did not change, but his eyes tracked the light.

When the sparklers died, the dark rushed back in, heavier than before. Harold dropped the hot wire onto the frozen ground and crushed it into the frost with his heel. Hiss. A tiny puff of steam rose and vanished.

They were standing close enough to share breath now. The smell of sulphur and burnt metal hung between them, acidic and sharp.

Harold opened his mouth. His lips parted. He looked as if he were about to say everything: about school, the football pitch, the fear, the piano.

But the wind picked up. It rattled the last dry leaves of the oak tree like bones.

The moment folded in on itself. It was too fragile to survive articulation. If they spoke, they might shatter it.

Harold closed his mouth. He hunched his shoulders, pulling the hoodie tighter. He turned away, toward the yellow rectangles of distant windows that marked the safety of his other life.

Patrick waited. He waited until the sound of Harold's crunching footsteps on the gravel vanished completely.

Only then did he allow himself to exhale.

The paper aeroplane was still in his pocket, damp now with the sweat of his palm. He left it there. It was a map of a country they might never visit again.

Patrick turned and walked home beneath the waning moon. Every step stamped a dark, temporary hole into the silver frost: evidence that he had been there, that they had been there, even if the morning sun would melt it all away before the first bell rang.

Chapter IV

Equations of the Heart

The autumn of 1991 did not arrive with fanfares; it slipped in unannounced, smelling of wet wool, cheap cider, and fresh photocopies.

Patrick stepped off the number 65 bus with a portfolio under his arm that felt less like an accessory and more like a shield. A headache throbbed behind his eyes, a souvenir of the previous night's farewell drinks pulsing to the rhythm of his heart. His mother's parting lullaby was still lodged in his ear, a frantic whisper delivered on the threshold as she adjusted his collar for the last time:

"Remember to eat something green, darling. Vegetables. And do not tell anyone too much about... you know."

Thames Valley University loomed before him. It was not the dreaming spires of Oxford nor the gothic grandeur of Durham he had read about in novels. It was a concrete experiment someone had abandoned mid-pour, a brutalist, assertive slab of grey against a sky the colour of dishwater. The rain made the pavement slick, turning the world into a blurred reflection of slate and neon.

Patrick stopped, letting the drizzle settle on his eyelashes. He adjusted the strap of his duffel bag, feeling the weight of his entire life shifted onto one shoulder.

This is it, he told himself. The beginning of another place.

Inside the art building, the air shifted. It smelled of turpentine, linseed oil, and a sharp desperation. Patrick navigated the corridor, the linoleum squeaking beneath his damp soles, nearly colliding with a trolley stacked with still-wet canvases that smelled of oil paint and possibility.

"Watch it, fresher!" barked the technician, a man with a beard that looked like a bird's nest and hands stained with Prussian blue.

Patrick muttered an apology, his pulse already fluttering like a trapped moth against his ribs. He found his assigned studio cubicle. It was a glorified cupboard: three walls of chipboard and a north-facing window that admitted a miserable square of grey sky.

He dropped his bag with a heavy thud. He pinned a single sheet of paper to the white wall. It was a charcoal smudge, a quick, violent sketch of a profile drawn from the uncertain distance of memory. Harold's nose. Harold's jaw.

Patrick sat on the floor, the cold seeping through his jeans. He hugged his knees to his chest, curled into himself, and waited for the trembling in his hands to subside. He was eighteen years old and felt as though he had been set adrift in open water without a compass.

Harold appeared at lunchtime, as if the charcoal sketch had conjured him from the ether.

He stood at the door of the cubicle, clutching a heavy plastic folder stuffed with papers. He looked different. His hair was shorter, the rebellious cowlick tamed with gel. He wore an ironed shirt, tucked into trousers that held a crisp, deliberate crease. He looked as though he were playing a role he had not yet fully memorized.

Patrick stood up too quickly. The blood pooled in his feet, making him dizzy, the room tilting for a second.

"Hello," Harold said.

The syllable landed softly, like a single snowflake on hot pavement.

"Hello," Patrick breathed.

"I saw your name on the registration list outside," Harold said, gesturing vaguely toward the corridor. "I thought... well."

"Yes."

"Do you want a coffee? The machine downstairs isn't too bad."

They walked to the dining hall. It was a cavernous space filled with the roar of a thousand conversations bouncing off the concrete walls. First-years were comparing their A-level results like poker hands, complaining about delays in their student loans, and posing with cigarettes held at awkward, practised angles.

Patrick and Harold bought coffee in polystyrene cups. It tasted of burnt rubber and powdered milk, a familiar, institutional comfort. They chose a table by the rain-streaked glass, as far from the noise as possible.

"What are you studying?" Patrick asked, blowing on the steam.

"Education," Harold said. He tapped the folder on the table. "With a focus on Politics and Law. They're sending us into classrooms before Christmas, for observation."

Harold's thumb worried the cardboard sleeve of his cup, picking at the seam until it frayed. It was a nervous tic Patrick remembered from the cinema, from the days of The NeverEnding Story.

"You?" Harold asked.

"Fine Arts."

Patrick smiled, a crooked and nervous thing.

"And we've got nude by Friday."

He meant Life Drawing classes. It was a standard art school joke. But it emerged raw, hanging suspended in the air with an accidental, flirtatious weight that neither of them was prepared for.

Colour flooded Harold's throat, rising from his neck like a tide. He choked on his coffee, coughing into his hand to hide his face.

"Right," Harold managed to say, his voice strangled. "Right. Nude. Of course."

Patrick looked away, mortified. He looked out the window and saw only his own reflection—greasy fringe, a charcoal smudge on his cheek like a bruise—superimposed on the grey campus beyond. He looked chaotic. Harold looked orderly. They were distinct species now, evolved for different environments.

The days assumed a cautious, syncopated rhythm.

They did not seek each other out. There was no plan, no schedule pinned to a fridge. Yet they collided with a magnetic and reliable strangeness.

They would meet at the library photocopier at 9:00 a.m., both sleep-deprived, watching the light scan back and forth like a heartbeat. They would meet on the footbridge at dusk, where the river below smelled of rust and duckweed, watching the swans navigate the current with effortless grace. They would meet in the launderette at midnight when the city folded into its quietest self, and the only sound was the rhythmic hum of the tumble dryers spinning the clothes.

Each encounter lasted the length of a cigarette, a dryer cycle, the walk between two buildings. They talked about essays and landlords. They complained about the damp in their halls of residence. They never talked about the sparklers. They never talked about holding hands. They never talked about the kiss that had almost happened, whose ghost still split their childhood in two.

October delivered its first hard frost. The temperature plummeted, turning the campus into a landscape of silver and grey.

Patrick's studio turned freezing. The heating in the art block was temperamental, rattling pipes that delivered no heat, only noise. The charcoal refused to adhere to the cold paper; it slipped off the grain like a reluctant confession, leaving faint, ghostly trails.

He gave up drawing. He worked instead with ink. He painted a series of nearly black squares, heavy and oppressive, interrupted by fine cracks of raw umber and gold.

His tutor, a woman named Sheila who wore formidable scarf combinations and smelled of cloves, prowled among the easels, her heels clicking like the ticktock of a countdown clock.

She stopped behind Patrick. She stared fixedly at the black square.

"And the figure? This is an evasion, Patrick. Where is the body?"

Patrick thought of Harold standing beneath the footbridge the night before, the negative space around his shoulders taking the exact shape of longing. He thought of the way Harold's coat wrinkled at the elbows, retaining his form even when he was not there.

"He left," Patrick replied, dipping his brush into the black ink. "He is no longer there."

Sheila snorted, adjusted her glasses, and moved on to critique a painting of a fruit bowl.

That night, the heating in the Halls of Residence failed completely.

The radiators gurgled and died. By 10:00 p.m., the temperature in the rooms was visible in the plumes of breath rising from the students' lips.

The students migrated to the dining hall, wrapping themselves in duvets like refugees. Someone produced a contraband kettle. Someone else found a bottle of own-brand rum. A guitar appeared. It became a carnival of shivering youth, a desperate party against the cold.

Patrick could not bear the noise. He could not bear the forced camaraderie, the performative warmth. He grabbed his box of pastels and walked to the library.

It was open 24 hours during term time. The heating was on.

He found Harold alone at a long table on the second floor. The table was strewn with papers, thick textbooks on Education Law, and highlighters in neon yellow and pink.

The fluorescent lights overhead hummed a low, electric lullaby of resistance. Mmmmmmm.

Patrick walked over to the table. He set down his box of pastels. They clattered, rolling like illicit sweets across the Formica.

Harold looked up. He looked exhausted. There were dark circles under his eyes, but when he saw Patrick, his face softened.

"Do you mind if I stay here to work?" Patrick asked. "My room is a fridge."

Harold smiled: a small, grateful expression that did not quite reach his eyes but warmed Patrick all the same.

"Please. It keeps me awake. Statutory instruments are better than any sleeping pill."

Patrick sat across from him. He opened his sketchbook. Harold returned to his reading.

They sat there for three hours. Each annotated his separate silence. Patrick sketched the curve of Harold's wrist as he wrote, capturing the tension in the tendons. Harold highlighted lines of text about the Education Act 1944.

At half-past twelve, Harold closed his book with a heavy thud. He flexed his fingers, which were stained yellow from the highlighters.

"I'm done."

Patrick looked up.

"Me too."

"Will you walk back with me?" Harold asked.

It was not really a question.

Outside, the frost had settled like powdered glass over every surface. The railings, the bins, the grass: everything glittered beneath the streetlamps, sharp and beautiful.

Their footsteps broke the thin crust, the sound intimate and magnified in the empty street. Crunch. Crunch.

At Harold's block, they stopped beneath a security light that buzzed and flickered, bathing them in harsh, intermittent white flashes.

Harold turned to look at him. His breath formed plumes in the freezing air. Patrick watched the cloud rise, dissipate, and felt time tilt on its axis.

"I have a seminar at nine," Harold said. His voice was low, dropping beneath the hum of the light. "But the Block B launderette opens at six. It's usually empty then. If you want... coffee."

The pause before the word coffee contained galaxies. It contained the weight of everything they were not saying.

Patrick's heart performed a clumsy, desperate pirouette in his chest. He nodded, shoving his hands deep into his coat pockets to hide his trembling. He did not trust language.

"Six," Patrick said.

"Six," Harold confirmed.

At ten to six the next morning, Patrick was sitting on a plastic chair in the launderette. He was surrounded by spinning machines. The air was thick with the smell of cheap detergent and the thunder of water.

He had charcoal dust under his fingernails and fresh paint on his wrist.

Harold arrived at exactly 6:00 a.m. He carried two chipped mugs emblazoned with the university crest. Steam rose from them.

"Hello," Harold said.

"Hello."

The coffee was instant. It was bitter. It was perfect.

They sat on the folding tables, legs dangling. They talked about legal cases: Harold explained the duty of care in schools. They talked about colour theory: Patrick explained why blue was the colour of distance. They talked about fathers who measured success in withheld praise and mothers who loved too anxiously.

When Harold's washing machine finally clicked and stopped, the sudden silence felt violent. It was like plunging into deep water. The white noise that had protected them was gone.

Patrick stood up to leave.

"I have to go. I have Life Drawing."

Harold stood up too.

When Patrick turned around, Harold reached out. He caught Patrick's wrist.

It was an instinctive gesture, clumsy and fast. Harold's fingers slipped across a patch of wet cobalt blue paint on Patrick's arm that Patrick had not noticed.

Harold did not let go. He held on for a second, his grip strong, an anchor against the drift.

"Stay," Harold said.

He looked at his hand. He looked at the blue paint now smeared across his own white cuff. A fingerprint of sky. A blue accusation against the white cotton.

Patrick looked at it too. He looked at Harold's face, which was open and terrified.

"I can't," Patrick whispered. "Not yet."

"All right," Harold said. He let go.

But Patrick did not leave. Not really. He sat back down on a tumble dryer that vibrated beneath him like a massive, purring animal.

"I'll stay for ten minutes," Patrick said.

So, he stayed. He watched Harold fold shirts with the precision of a lawyer, smoothing out the wrinkles. Neither mentioned the blue mark on Harold's cuff. Harold did not try to wash it off. He buttoned the sleeve, hiding the mark against his skin, preserving it.

They began to borrow time in earnest.

They carved out pockets of existence where the rules of the outside world did not apply.

Sunday dawns in the printmaking room, where the smell of ink and solvents was dizzying. Harold read the Sunday papers while Patrick cleaned the lithography stones.

Wednesday dusks on the river path, where the weeping willows trailed in the water. Harold recited contract cases—Carlill v Carbolic Smoke Ball Co—and Patrick responded with pigment recipes—Bone black, burnt sienna, alizarin crimson.

Friday midnights in the chapel cloisters, sharing a bottle of cheap red wine that stained their mouths purple. Their whispers returned to them from the stone arches like homing pigeons.

Harold learned to tell cadmium from vermilion. Patrick learned the Latin roots of mens rea.

They did not kiss.

Although once, laughing at something stupid, they bumped foreheads. The laughter stopped instantly. For three suspended heartbeats, they breathed the same small parcel of air. Patrick could smell the soap Harold used. He could see the dilation of Harold's pupils.

A cleaner coughed around the corner, dragging a mop bucket.

The spell shattered. They pulled apart, their pulses beating wildly, staring at the floor.

November stripped the trees down to charcoal scribbles again.

Patrick's final submission for the term was due. He had created twelve panels exploring "Negative Space". They hung in the studio like open windows into the night. Black squares. Blue voids.

In the largest piece, he had done something secret.

He had embedded a single thread of blue wool. It was from Harold's scarf, unravelled during a night walk when it had snagged on a bramble. Patrick had kept it.

He sealed the thread beneath layers of translucent gesso and white glaze. It was invisible unless you knew where to look. A blue curve arching, ghostly, across the white void.

He titled it Equation #1.

When the assessment panel came through, they were baffled.

"It is very... minimal," his tutor said. "What is the equation solving?"

Patrick stood with his arms crossed, feeling the ghost of the thread humming in the paint.

"It is solving for distance," he said.

On the last day of term, they left campus on the same bus.

The National Express to London. They sat across the aisle from one another. The luggage racks groaned with portfolios and duffel bags.

The sky over Reading was the colour of dirty dishwater. Sleet tapped against the windows: tick, tick, tick.

Patrick pressed his forehead against the cold glass. He felt the vibration of the engine in his teeth.

He looked at the reflection in the window. He could see Harold's face floating there, superimposed over the passing grey suburbs. Ghost Harold.

Their eyes met in the glass. Real and not real.

They held the gaze.

Harold's eyelids dropped first, closing over some private calculation. He looked tired. He looked as though he were holding something heavy he could not let go of.

The bus exhaled its air brakes and pulled onto the motorway. London unravelled before them, an unwritten manuscript.

Between them, the aisle remained. It was narrow enough to touch across. It was wide enough to drown in.

Neither of them leaned across. Not yet.

But the possibility lived there, in the space between the seats. It was patient. It was waiting, like roots beneath the snow, waiting for the thaw that had to arrive eventually.

∞∞∞

Chapter V

Shattered Silence

The call arrived on a Thursday the colour of wet ash.

It was late October 1998. Patrick was in his Brooklyn studio, a converted warehouse space that smelled of turpentine, old coffee, and the Hudson River. He was mixing Payne's Grey with a whisper of Alizarin Crimson, trying to capture the specific, bruised purple of a shadow he had seen on the subway that morning.

The telephone rang. It was a landline; a bulky plastic thing covered in paint splatters, an artifact in a room dedicated to the present moment.

He picked it up with his left hand, keeping the paintbrush balanced in his right, protecting the delicate equilibrium of the pigment.

"Hello?"

The voice on the other end was the department secretary from his father's old engineering firm in London. Her voice was soft, muffled by the static of the Atlantic Ocean and the weight of a rehearsed condolence.

"Patrick? It's Mrs. Gable. I... I'm afraid I have bad news."

Patrick stopped breathing. The paintbrush in his hand suddenly felt heavy, like a lead pipe dragging his arm down.

"It's your father, dear. He passed away last night. It was... well, they say the heart. Quietly. Without drama."

Without drama. The words floated in the air, absurd and inadequate. His father, a man who had lived his life by the slide rule and the timetable, had simply decided to clock out early, leaving the ledger unbalanced.

The paintbrush slipped from Patrick's fingers. It hit the concrete floor with a wet slap, leaving a comet of dark pigment across the grey sealant. It looked like a bruise. It looked like a mistake that no one would think to clean up for months.

"Patrick? Are you there?"

"I am here," Patrick whispered, his voice sounding thin and strange in the large room. "I am coming home."

By evening, he was on a red-eye flight to Heathrow.

The cabin lights were dimmed to a pharmaceutical glow, a sickly apricot hue that made everyone look like wax figures. Patrick sat in window seat 34A, his forehead pressed against the cold plastic.

He kept waiting for the shock to bloom into tears. He waited for the shaking shoulders, the ragged breathing, the cinematic release of grief. But it did not arrive. Instead, his body hummed. He felt as though someone had unscrewed the top of his skull and poured in liquid nitrogen. He was cold, crystalline, and utterly numb.

He watched England assemble itself beneath the plane in the pre-dawn light. The patchwork fields were dark squares of green and brown; the sodium streetlamps were necklaces of orange beads; the M25 motorway was a luminous bracelet jammed with early-morning lorries.

He felt nothing. Not nostalgia. Not sadness. Only the phantom weight of a sensation from years ago: Harold's hand on his wrist in a university launderette, three thousand miles and a lifetime away.

Stay, the ghost whispered.

I cannot, Patrick thought. I am already gone.

Harold heard the news from Carole, who had heard it from Patrick's mother in the cheese aisle of Waitrose.

Harold was standing in the kitchen of his terraced house in Hammersmith. It was Saturday morning. The radio was playing Classic FM, a calm, orderly soundtrack for a calm, orderly life.

He was spreading marmalade on toast. He held the knife with the precision of a man who now drafted contracts for a living, ensuring an even distribution.

"Pat's dad died," Carole said over the telephone. "Heart attack."

The knife stopped mid-swipe. It skidded across the toast, leaving a bright orange smear on the white plate.

Harold stared at the marmalade. He felt the air leave the room, vacuumed away by the news.

"When?" Harold asked.

"Thursday night. Patrick is flying in."

Harold wanted to hang up the phone. He wanted to drive to Ealing. He wanted to call Patrick immediately. He wanted to do something appropriately adult: send flowers, order a wreath, write a card on thick cream stationery.

But every phrase that came to mind felt obscene. Deepest sympathies. Thinking of you. Those were phrases for colleagues, for distant relatives. They were not phrases for the boy who had helped him build a lunar city in a lilac bush.

He hung up the phone. He looked at his hands. He had marmalade under his fingernail. He tried to type a text message on his Nokia.

I am so sorry, Pat.

He looked at the screen. It seemed cold. He deleted the comma. He deleted the name. Then he deleted the entire message.

He went to work in his study with the marmalade still under his fingernail, a tiny, sticky reminder of a world that had just stopped turning.

The funeral was set for Tuesday at St. Stephen's.

It was the red brick church that had defined the geography of their childhood. It was where they had sung Christmas carols in itchy woollen jumpers; it was where they had attended harvest festivals holding tins of baked beans.

Patrick arrived early. He was jet-lagged; his internal clock screaming that it was 4:00 a.m.

He was not prepared for how small the building appeared. It was as if someone had left the church in a hot wash for too long and it had shrunk. The vaulted ceiling felt lower. The stained-glass windows seemed dimmer.

The undertaker, a man who moved with the silent efficiency of a butler, guided Patrick to a side pew.

"Family here, sir," he murmured.

Patrick sat down. The air tasted of brass polish, damp stone, and lilies: cloyingly sweet, heavy with pollen. It was the scent of endings.

He sat with his knees locked together, his hands gripping his thighs. His mother sat beside him, wrapped in black wool, looking like a shattered bird held together by pins.

The organist was rehearsing a Bach prelude. He kept stumbling on the same minor chord. Da-da-DUM... silence... Da-da-DUM.

Each repetition felt like a question Patrick could not answer. Are you all right? Are you all right?

The doors at the back of the church opened. A gust of damp wind blew inside, making the candles flicker.

Patrick did not turn around. He watched the reflection in the polished brass of the lectern.

He saw a figure enter.

Harold.

He wore a navy-blue overcoat, the collar turned up against the November drizzle. He had not been included on the official list of mourners. He had not been invited. He had simply come.

He slipped into the back row, next to Carole. Patrick watched in the curved reflection as Carole reached out and took Harold's hand. Harold did not look at her. His eyes were fixed on the back of Patrick's head.

Patrick felt his spine uncoil for the first time in three days. The buzzing in his head quietened. Harold was here. The architecture of the world, which had collapsed on Thursday, reassembled itself slightly. Harold was the load-bearing wall.

The service unfolded in polite, Anglican increments. A psalm about green pastures. A eulogy read by an uncle that listed professional achievements but omitted the man. A hymn chosen for its appropriately melancholic shift in tone.

"Change and decay in all around I see..."

Patrick sang mechanically. His voice was thin, reedy. It cracked on the high note of "decay".

Behind him, three rows back, a baritone rose.

It was rich, deep, and steady. It enveloped Patrick's tenuous tenor like a warm blanket. It covered the break in his voice. Harold was singing. He was singing the harmony line, the one he had learned in the choir when they were twelve.

"O Thou who changest not, abide with me."

The sound vibrated through the wooden pew. It held Patrick up.

When the final "Amens" settled, the congregation stood. There was a rustling of heavy coats and swallowed grief.

Patrick turned. He wanted to catch Harold's eye. He wanted to nod.

But Harold was already moving. He was retreating down the side aisle, head bowed, moving fast. Too early. Too much. Too late.

Outside, the sky had lowered to the colour of wet slate.

Patrick stood beneath a canvas awning that drummed with the rain. Dram-dram-dram. He accepted condolences. He shook hands with men his father had worked with men with firm grips and wandering eyes who wanted to be anywhere else.

"He was a good man," they would say.

"Thank you," Patrick would say.

"A solid man."

"Yes."

Every handshake left a ghost of dampness on his palm. Every platitude landed like a pebble thrown against the window of a house that was already empty.

When the last mourner had drifted away toward the car park, Patrick turned back to the roofed porch.

Harold was waiting.

He stood beside the old yew hedge; his hands shoved deep into the pockets of that navy-blue overcoat, a coat Patrick did not recognize. It was an adult's coat. Expensive wool.

Patrick walked over. The gravel crunched beneath his black Oxford shoes.

Harold looked up. The rain jewelled his eyelashes. He did not blink.

"I am not good at this," Harold said. His voice was rough. "I never know what to do with death. With death there are no rules."

Patrick almost laughed. It was an involuntary hiccup of sound that hurt his chest.

"No one does, H. We simply carry it with us until it learns to walk on its own."

They stood in the thin shelter of the yew. The traffic on Uxbridge Road hissed past, tyres on wet tarmac. A funeral party from the crematorium next door filed past them: a line of black umbrellas blooming like bruises against the grey sky.

Patrick shivered. The cold was seeping through his suit, settling into his marrow.

Harold moved. He unwound his scarf. It was grey cashmere, soft as dust. He took a step forward.

He did not ask. He simply looped it once, twice, around Patrick's neck. He tucked the ends in with gentle, efficient fingers.

The gesture brought them closer than polite society allowed. For a second, Patrick was enveloped in Harold's personal atmosphere. He smelled of wet wool. He smelled of the faint, bitter tang of marmalade. And beneath that, the cedarwood scent of a cologne Patrick knew Harold had not chosen for himself.

Patrick closed his eyes. He wanted to lean in. He wanted to bury his face in the rough wool of the navy overcoat. He wanted to say: Stay. Come back. Do not ever leave me again.

But what emerged was smaller. Safer.

"Will you walk me home?" Patrick asked.

Harold stepped back, his hands returning to his pockets.

"Yes. Of course."

They took the long route.

They passed through the park where the horse chestnut tree had once served as a bridge over the stream. It was gone now. Cut down by the council, the stump sealed with black tar like a cauterized wound.

They passed the corner shop, which was now a Tesco Express, its bright branding glaring against the muted street.

Frost had begun to lace the puddles on the pavement. Their footsteps shattered the thin ice. Crack. Crack.

Harold talked. He filled the silence with safe, rectangular topics. He talked about his law firm's move to new offices in the city ("glass and steel, soulless"). He talked about the housing market.

"And Sarah," Harold said, hesitating on the name. "My daughter. She is three. She is... loud. She wants a drum kit."

Patrick felt a small, sharp pinch in his side. A daughter. A life. A drum kit.

"Drum kits are good," Patrick said, his voice neutral. "Better than silence."

"I suppose."

Harold looked at him.

"The Thames smells of rust when the tide goes out near our house. I hate it. It reminds me of the footbridge at Uni."

Patrick looked at him sharply.

"I thought you liked that bridge."

"I liked who I was on it," Harold said quietly.

They walked in silence for a block. Patrick's concentration was swallowed by the simple, overwhelming fact of having Harold by his side. The swing of their arms occasionally brushed wool against wool. A Morse code of proximity.

When they reached the junction where their childhoods had always bifurcated—left for Patrick's house, right for Harold's—Patrick stopped.

He looked at the street sign.

"I keep thinking I should feel something larger," Patrick said. He looked at his hands. "A crater. An explosion. Instead, it is just... a dent. As if someone sat heavily on a sofa and got up again, and the cushion hasn't sprung back into place."

Harold turned to him. He pulled his hand from his pocket. He was wearing leather gloves.

He reached out and took Patrick's bare hand. He threaded their fingers together without ceremony. The leather was cold, but the grip was iron.

"Grief is not a hole, Patrick," Harold said. He looked directly into Patrick's eyes. "It is a room. A room you keep walking into. Some days the switch works. Others it doesn't. And you just have to stand in the dark and wait."

The metaphor landed softly, with the exact weight. It was an architect's grief. Structural. Bearable.

Patrick squeezed Harold's hand. Once. Recognition. Gratitude. Love.

He let go before the moment could demand a translation, he was not ready to give.

They reached the door of Patrick's parents' house. The windows were half-lit, the curtains drawn. A single lamp burned in the hallway like a watchful eye.

Patrick fished his key from his pocket. The metal bit into his palm.

"Do you want to come in?" Patrick asked. "Mum has a million casseroles. People keep bringing lasagne. We could heat up... something."

Harold looked at the house. He looked at the window where Patrick's father used to sit and read the newspaper.

"Another day," Harold said.

The word day hung suspended in the air. It carried enough promise to warm three blocks of winter. It implied that there would be other days.

Harold turned to leave. Then he stopped. He turned back.

"Wait," Harold said. "I brought this."

He dug into the deep pocket of his overcoat. He pulled out a small, rectangular metal tin.

It was a Winsor & Newton watercolour set. The black enamel kind. It was battered, scratched, the edges showing silver where the paint had worn away.

Patrick took it. The metal retained the faint heat of Harold's body.

He opened it. Twelve half-pans of colour. They were barely used, but they were there. Cerulean. Burnt Sienna. Viridian.

"I found it in my desk," Harold said. "I must have... I don't know. Grabbed it by mistake years ago. Or kept it. I thought you might... need colours. Everything is so grey right now."

Patrick looked at the paints. He thought of the nights in Brooklyn when he had mixed paint with tears. He thought of canvases heavy as coffin lids.

"Thank you," Patrick whispered.

Then, because the day had already broken all the rules, Patrick leaned forward.

He kissed Harold's cheek.

It was quick. Dry. The scratch of cold skin, the roughness of stubble, and the taste of rain.

Harold did not move. He did not pull away.

His eyes closed. For the duration of a heartbeat, two, he leaned into the touch.

When Patrick stepped back, the space between them felt altered. It was no longer empty. It was charged, as if an invisible thread had been threaded through both their chests and pulled taut.

"Go inside, Pat," Harold said softly.

Harold turned and walked away. He did not look back.

Patrick stood at the door. He watched the navy overcoat retreat down the street, turning the corner into the dusk, fading into the London fog.

Only then did he go inside.

The house smelled of lilies and his mother's perfume, which had gone stale. The silence was thick.

Patrick climbed the stairs to his old bedroom. It was exactly as he had left it at eighteen. Posters of bands that no longer existed.

He walked to the window. He placed the paint tin on the sill.

He opened the lid again.

Inside the white enamel of the lid, written in pencil, so faint it could have been a trick of the light, was Harold's handwriting.

For the dawn, when it arrives.

Patrick stared at the words.

Outside, the rain eased into a mist that softened every edge of the suburbs. Somewhere in the distance, a siren doppler away. Elsewhere, a dog barked once, then thought better of it.

Patrick stood for a long time, his palm resting on the cold metal of the paint tin. He felt the faint pulse of retained heat fading to room temperature, but he knew the colours were there.

When he finally slept that night, fully clothed on top of his duvet, he dreamed of footsteps shattering the frost. He dreamed of a scarf that smelled of cedar and safety. He dreamed of a room where the light switch flickered, buzzed, and threatened to fail, but stubbornly, miraculously, refused to go dark.

Chapter VI

Brushstrokes of Becoming

Patrick landed at JFK on a January morning in 1999 that smelled of jet fuel, burnt coffee, and wet asphalt.

He was twenty-six years old, but he felt ancient, as if the flight across the Atlantic had aged him a decade for every time zone crossed.

Customs glanced at his paint-stained fingers—Prussian blue trapped in the cuticles, impossible to scrub away—and waved him through with a bored stamp.

Outside the terminal, the air was violent. It was so cold it burned the lining of his nose, a sharp, chemical cold that felt nothing like the penetrating damp of London. The snow had been shovelled into grey, calcified banks along the curb, stained with exhaust fumes like dirty bandages. He hailed a yellow cab, wrestling his portfolio against a wind that threatened to tear it from his hands.

"School of Visual Arts, 23rd Street," he told the driver through the scratched Plexiglas partition.

He watched Queens unspool beyond the window. It was not the polite brick of Ealing. It was a chaotic sprawl of industrial walls tattooed with graffiti, water towers perched on rooftops like alien tripods, and neon signs blinking against a sky the colour of dishwater. It was ugly, and it was exhilarating.

The dorm room on 24th Street smelled of instant noodle soup, cheap deodorant, and fresh plywood.

His roommate was a boy from Oregon named Rook. Rook wore only black, smoked clove cigarettes indoors despite the smoke detectors, and quoted William Burroughs as if it were sacred scripture.

"Existence is a collage," Rook declared, as if it were a physical law, gesturing with a lit cigarette.

Then he vanished for three days, leaving behind only the lingering scent of cloves and mystery.

Patrick unpacked slowly. He had brought truly little. Two sketchbooks. Four sweaters that would prove useless against the wind tunnel of the Manhattan avenues. And the tin of Winsor & Newton watercolours that Harold had slipped into his coat pocket at the funeral.

He placed the tin on the windowsill. The winter light slid across the battered black metal like a cautious cat. He touched the lid. It was cold.

Orientation was a blur of welcome packets and bad coffee in paper cups that leaked through the seams.

The professors spoke in quiet, deliberate sentences, pacing the lecture halls in black turtlenecks. They spoke as if art were a controlled substance, something dangerous that required a licence to handle.

"You are here to dismantle your history," a sculpture professor announced, leaning over the podium. "You are here to forget where you come from."

They assigned projects designed to crack them open. Map your inner city. Paint the sound of your own breathing. Create a self-portrait without showing your face.

Patrick began at 2:00 a.m. on a Tuesday. The heating in the dorm room clanked like a dying engine. He used the radiator as an easel because the room was too small for anything else.

The first canvas emerged a bruised purple. He slashed it with fissures of pitch black, dragging the palette knife through the wet paint until the canvas screamed. It looked like a broken vein. It looked like the map of a pain he had not admitted to feeling.

He titled it *Equation #2*.

He turned it to face the wall so he would not have to meet its gaze.

The days took on a cadence, a staccato rhythm different from the adagio of London.

Morning critiques, where students tore each other apart with polysyllabic words. Afternoon studio, smelling of turpentine and linseed oil. Nights spent walking the city's grid, searching for warmer socks and a silence that did not exist.

He learned to buy coffee at the bodega on Second Avenue. The cashier, a man named Sal who blasted opera at full volume, called him "English" and let him owe fifty cents when he was short on change.

He learned the subway map the way sailors once learned the stars. A, C, E. Red line downtown. Transfer at West Fourth.

He learned that snow could fall upward in New York. When the wind scolded the avenues between the glass towers, the flakes swirled and rose, defying gravity, returning to the sky that had rejected them.

In February, the university organized a group exhibition for the MFA students.

Patrick submitted a triptych. Three panels of nearly black gesso scraped and sanded so heavily they looked like frost on the window of an abandoned warehouse.

Into the central panel, he had worked a single strand of grey wool. It was from the cashmere scarf Harold had given him at the funeral. It was invisible from a distance. You had to step closer. You had to let the raking light catch it. It was Harold's ghost, travelling across an ocean, buried in the paint.

During the opening, people walked right past it. They were looking for the "figure." They were looking for the "narrative." They saw nothing but black.

Except for one person.

A second-year sculpture student named Nek stood in front of the triptych for ten minutes. She was small, fierce, dressed in a white men's shirt buttoned to the throat and smelling faintly of cedar shavings and tobacco.

She turned to Patrick, who was hovering near the cheap wine, trying to disappear into the white wall.

"You have someone tucked into that painting," she said. It was not a question. Her voice was raspy, certain.

Patrick felt the floor tilt. He squeezed his plastic cup until it cracked.

"More or less," he murmured.

Nek nodded. She did not press.

"Come on. There's too much noise in here."

She led him to the fire escape. They stood on the metal grating, the city groaning beneath them like a restless sleeper. Sleet tapped against the iron stairs. *Tick-tick-tick*.

Nek lit a cigarette and offered him one.

She told him her mother had come from Oaxaca. She told him that colour was a form of inheritance.

"Some pigments come from insects," she said, blowing smoke into the sleet, "like cochineal. And others are ground from the bones of saints. Or so my grandmother used to say, that they came from the bones of saints. Everything comes from a body, Patrick. Even paint."

Patrick listened. His throat felt raw. He realized, standing there in the freezing drizzle, that he had not spoken aloud about home—about the feeling of home—since leaving Heathrow.

"I am painting a ghost," Patrick confessed.

Nek looked at him. Her eyes were dark, ancient.

"We all are. Just make sure the ghost pays rent."

Spring arrived sideways.

One afternoon, he found a flyer taped to his dorm room door: LIFE DRAWING MARATHON. 24 HOURS. NON-STOP MODEL. PIZZA PROVIDED.

He went. He told himself it was for the discipline. Mostly, it was for the pizza.

The studio was hot. The model was a woman in her sixties. She had silver hair that fell to her waist and a mastectomy scar on her left side that she refused to hide. She sat on the podium with the regality of a queen.

The other students sketched frantically. Patrick could see them hesitating. They were afraid of the scar. They were afraid of their own inability to name it with charcoal. They drew around it, smoothing the skin, correcting the body.

Patrick drew the scar first.

He drew it as a pale, decisive lightning bolt across the continent of her chest. He drew the way the skin pulled taut around it. Then he drew the soft weight of her belly, the quiet authority of her hips, the heavy fall of her hair.

In the fourteenth hour, his stick of charcoal snapped. *Crack*.

He did not stop. He continued with the broken stump, his fingers blistered, smudging the black dust into the paper.

He entered a trance-like state. The room dissolved. The smell of pizza and sweat faded into a grey hum.

When the timer finally rang to mark the end, Patrick blinked. He looked down at his paper.

He had drawn the woman. But emerging from the shadow of her shoulder, formed by the negative space of her hair, was a profile.

A nose. A jawline. A rebellious cowlick.

Harold.

It was unmistakable. As if the paper itself had decided to confess what Patrick's hand refused to admit.

He pinned the drawing above his bed that night.

Rook looked at it as he packed a bag for another mysterious disappearance.

"You're fucked up, man," Rook said, shaking his head.

Then he left.

Patrick slept for twelve straight hours.

When he woke, he had the taste of turpentine in his mouth. He walked to Washington Square Park. He sat on the concrete edge of the fountain. It was dry, filled with dead leaves and rubbish.

Skateboards clattered nearby. Pigeons plotted a coup around a discarded loaf of bread. The marble arch rose white and indifferent against a wind-scoured sky.

Patrick opened his sketchbook. He uncapped his fountain pen.

He wrote a single line:

I am painting myself into existence without you.

He stared at the words. They felt true. They felt like a betrayal.

He tore the page out. He folded it carefully into a paper boat. A shape from childhood.

He set it sailing in a puddle of rainwater at the bottom of the fountain.

He watched the ink bleed. He watched the paper dissolve into pulp before it reached the far edge.

Money became a religion he could not afford to practise.

His savings were gone. He took a job at a coffee shop on East Ninth Street. It was a shoebox of a place that played jazz and smelled of roasted beans.

He spent his days with espresso grounds embedded beneath his fingernails. He steamed milk until the machine shrieked.

The manager, a failed actor named Sal (a different Sal from the bodega), told him, "Smile like you mean it, English. We sell coffee and theatre here."

Patrick practised the smile in the stainless-steel reflection of the pastry case. It came out crooked, a little broken.

"It'll do," Sal said. "Crooked looks real. People like real."

Between shifts, Patrick painted.

He painted on the floor of his room, the radiator clanking like a bad heart. The work became looser. He stopped trying to be precise. He stopped trying to be an architect.

He let the paint drip. He let the gestures abandon themselves in the air. He chose colours by instinct: cadmium orange, cerulean blue, a violent crimson.

One canvas depicted a boy on a bicycle. The figure was silhouetted against a sky the exact colour of Harold's old school scarf: navy-blue and grey. But the front wheel of the bicycle was not a wheel. It was dissolving into a flock of red birds scattering beyond the frame of the canvas.

He titled it *Escape Velocity*.

He hung it in the student gallery for the end-of-year review. He did not put a price tag on it.

Nek showed up at the opening. She carried a bottle of mezcal and two plastic cups.

"You are getting lighter," she said, pouring a generous measure.

"Am I?"

"Yes. The black is breaking apart. Soon you'll float."

They drank on the fire escape again. The traffic sighed up Second Avenue, a river of red taillights flowing north.

"I found a studio," Nek said. "In Chelsea. Converted warehouse. Raw brick. Freight elevator. Rats the size of theology students."

Patrick laughed. The mezcal burned pleasantly in his chest.

"Come paint with me," she said. "Bring your ghosts. We'll charge them rent."

He went the following weekend.

The space was cavernous. It smelled of cedar blocks (Nek's sculptures) and turpentine (Patrick's paint). It smelled of distances that were still possible.

He set up his easel by the window.

He painted until dawn. The radiator was a dull red sun at his back.

Sometime in the night, Nek draped a wool blanket over his shoulders. At another point, she placed a cup of coffee by his foot. He did not drink it until the paint on his brush had dried into a skin.

When the sun finally dragged itself over the East River, turning the water into molten copper, Patrick stepped back.

He saw what he had done.

A large canvas. It was divided in half.

The left side was deep, velvety blue: a London night. The right side was pale, bruised pink: a Manhattan dawn.

Connecting them, leaping the gap like an electrical arc, was a single red thread. It was painted with one fluid stroke of the brush.

It was a lifeline.

He signed it in the corner: *P. Evans, 1999*.

For the first time, the future tense settled in his chest. *I will be.*

Back in the dorm room, he found a letter leaning against the watercolour tin on his windowsill.

The envelope bore British stamps. His mother's careful, looping handwriting.

He opened it.

Inside was a pressed sprig of lavender from the garden in Ealing. It was dry, brittle. A photograph of his father's garden bench, wearing a patina of snow.

And a note. Three lines.

We are proud of you. The cold is kind. Come home when you are ready.

Patrick placed the lavender between the pages of his sketchbook. It stained the paper the pale violet of early memory.

Summer unfolded. Humid, orchestral, suffocating.

He quit the coffee shop. He took a weekend job at a Midtown gallery run by an energetic woman named Elena who wore architectural glasses.

"You have an eye," Elena told him. "And you can write."

She had him write press releases. He learned to turn adjectives into currency. "The artist explores absence as a measurable substance..." "A dialogue between memory and materiality..."

He listened to himself speaking with collectors and wondered who this "artist" was. Would Harold recognize him beneath the jargon? Would Harold look at *Escape Velocity* and see the bicycle they used to ride toward the Common?

One night in August, Patrick took the subway to the end of the line. Coney Island.

He walked along the boardwalk. The air smelled of salt, fried dough, and old wood.

The fairground rides threw neon light across the black water. The Wonder Wheel. The Cyclone. Couples screamed in manufactured terror as the roller coasters plunged.

Patrick bought a paper cup of beer and walked down to the sand.

He sat near the waterline. The tide washed up, erasing his footprints instantly.

He thought about writing. He thought about sending an email. Or a postcard.

Dear Harold, I am here. I am painting the scar. I don't know how to end this.

Instead, he pulled out his phone. He scrolled to the number he had never deleted. *H. Mobile.*

He let his thumb hover over the call button.

The moon hung over the Atlantic. It looked like a thin silver coin dropped through a slot in the sky that refused to yield its prize.

He did not press the button. He let the screen time out. The light faded to black.

He returned to the warehouse at dawn.

Nek was already there. She was printing giant woodcuts of monarch butterflies, pressing the black ink into the paper with a heavy roller. *Thump-swish. Thump-swish.*

She did not look up.

"You're late," she said, smiling.

"Traffic on the boardwalk," Patrick lied.

He went to his easel. He picked up his palette knife.

He mixed a colour he had never mixed before. A coral blush. A specific, fleeting pink that existed only for the duration of a dawn over the East River.

He applied it to the canvas. He scraped it off. He applied it again.

The canvas breathed.

Outside, the delivery trucks on the avenue coughed to life. Inside, the city was still small enough to fit inside a single room that smelled of turpentine, cedar, and becoming.

∞∞∞

Chapter VII

Worlds in Colour

Patrick left New York in the spring of 2001. He left with a single suitcase that had a broken zip, a stack of heavy, virgin sketchbooks, and a grant cheque folded inside a plastic Muji wallet.

The cheque was from a foundation Elena had applied to on his behalf. It was modest: just enough for hostels that smelled of bleach, for beans eaten straight from tins, and for bus tickets that smelled of diesel and the driver's coffee. But in his pocket, it felt like a key. It felt as if someone had slid it across a table and whispered: *Open anything.*

He took the Amtrak south from Penn Station. The train rocked him out of the city, through the industrial scar tissue of New Jersey, and down into the coal towns of Pennsylvania. He watched through the scratched glass as the hills were shaved into terraces, the earth laid bare in strips of grey and ochre, exposed like muscle beneath skin.

He crossed the Mississippi at Memphis. The river was a muscle of water, the colour of weak tea and deep history, moving with a deceptive, sluggish power that suggested it could swallow a city without choking.

In New Orleans, the humidity hit him like a physical embrace. He rented a room above a bakery on the edge of the French Quarter. Every dawn, the smell of fried dough and powdered sugar pumped through the floorboards, mingling with the scent of the river: mud, algae, and salt.

He spent his days on Royal Street. He painted the trumpet players who stood on the corners, their cheeks silvered with sweat, their instruments battered brass extensions of their own lungs.

One afternoon, he sketched an old man named Moses. Moses had eyes that were milky with cataracts but saw everything.

"Are you getting the blue right?" Moses asked, without looking at the canvas.

Patrick paused, his brush hovering.

"I am trying."

"The secret to cobalt," Moses said, tapping the valve of his trumpet with a calloused finger, "is to remember the sky right before a hurricane hits. It ain't a happy blue, son. It's a warning."

Patrick wrote that on the inside back cover of his sketchbook. *Cobalt is a warning.* He underlined it twice.

From Louisiana, he took the Greyhound west.

Texas was endless. The Houston dusk smelled of chemical refineries and sweet gardenias: a perfume of industry and nature fighting to a draw. San Antonio was a blinding white heat, where the Alamo seemed smaller than its legend, like a childhood hero measured with adult eyes.

Patrick drew constantly. He drew with a biro on napkins in roadside diners. He drew on ticket stubs. He drew on the blank backs of placemats that still bore the ghost of ketchup stains.

Outside El Paso, the bus broke down.

The engine died with a mechanical cough, leaving them stranded on the hard shoulder of a highway that stretched into infinity. The heat was absolute. The tarmac shimmered, liquefying the horizon. The other passengers huddled in the shade of the vehicle, fanning themselves with magazines.

Patrick walked away from the bus. He sat cross-legged on the gravel shoulder. The stones were hot enough to burn through his jeans.

He opened his paint box. He painted the horizon. It was not a line; it was a vibration. It was a razor edge of heat where Mexico floated like a rumour in the distance.

A lorry driver pulled over to check on them. He was a giant of a man with a face like a topographical map, weathered and creased.

"You are waiting for someone to come save you?" the lorry driver asked, shouting over the wind, looking at Patrick's easel.

"Something like that," Patrick said.

"I'm heading to Tucson. If you can fit that gear in the cab, I'll give you a lift."

Patrick climbed in. The cab smelled of stale tobacco and pine air freshener. The driver's name was Ray.

"Will you draw me a picture?" Ray asked after an hour of silence. "My wife says I never smile. I want to send her proof."

Patrick did it in charcoal on newsprint. It took thirty minutes, the wind whipping the paper against the clipboard as they drove with the windows rolled down. He drew the crags of Ray's face, the set of his jaw, and the ghost of a smile in the corner of his eye.

Ray looked at it. He nodded. He taped the drawing to his dashboard with masking tape.

"He's going to watch the road for me," Ray said.

He insisted on giving Patrick five dollars. Patrick kept the note in his shoe for three months, until the paper turned soft as fabric and the ink of the president's face dissolved with the sweat of his sole.

In Santa Fe, the light changed. It became thinner, higher, sharper, exposing every flaw and every beauty.

He stayed with Elena's cousin, a potter named Luz. She lived in an adobe house at the end of a dirt road, surrounded by piñon pines that smelled of resin in the sun.

Luz was small and fierce, with hands that were permanently stained with red clay. She fired her pieces in an outdoor kiln she fed with wood. At night, the kiln glowed like a captured small planet, breathing sparks into the desert sky.

"You paint like a European," Luz told him one morning, watching him mix a tube of green.

"I am one."

"You paint the air as if it holds water. Here, the air is thirsty. Look at the shadows. They are not grey: they are purple."

She taught him to see. She taught him that adobe was not beige but dawn pink, bruised plum, the exact shade of the inside of a dove's wing.

She took him to her neighbour, an old man who ground his own pigments. Patrick spent a week there, learning the chemistry of the earth. He ground malachite for green until his palms blistered. He scraped rust from old nails to make ochre. He crushed lapis lazuli for a blue that cost more than gold.

The colour entered his bloodstream. He blew his nose and saw vermilion dust. He washed his hands and the water ran turquoise.

They drove to Taos Pueblo before dawn. The air was freezing. When the sun crowned the mountains, the sky peeled back.

It revealed a strip of turquoise so pure, so violent, it felt like an intrusion to look at it.

Patrick painted it in three strokes. *Slash. Slash. Slash.*

Then he closed the sketchbook. He was afraid that if he kept painting, he would ruin the silence.

Mexico came next.

The border at Laredo was a bridge of buzzing fluorescents and bureaucracy. The officials spoke English with the same clipped cadence as his primary school teachers in Ealing.

But on the other side, the air changed instantly. It was thicker. It was scented with diesel, roasting sweetcorn, and damp earth. The light lowered, becoming golden and forgiving.

He travelled on third-class trains where the seats were wooden slats. Chickens nested in the overhead racks. Old women wrapped tamales in newspaper and offered them to him without asking his name, watching him eat with dark, satisfied eyes.

In San Miguel de Allende, he rented a room for a month. It opened onto a courtyard choked with bougainvillea and broken tiles.

His landlady, Señora Álvarez, wore black. She had worn black since 1961.

"My husband," she told Patrick, pouring him sweet coffee. "He left forty years ago."

"That is a long time to mourn," Patrick said softly.

She shook her head.

"Colour is a courtesy to the living, Patricio. And I have no one left to dress in colour for."

Patrick painted her hands one afternoon. He painted the blue cords of her veins, the silver rings that had grown loose, the knuckles swollen like knots in driftwood.

When he showed it to her, she did not speak. She touched the painted hands with her real ones. She wept soundlessly, her shoulders shaking in the quiet of the kitchen.

He moved south. Oaxaca.

He found a room in a weaver's compound. The master weaver was a woman named Lety. Her loom clattered like rain on a tin roof, a rhythmic heartbeat that began at dawn and did not stop until dusk. *Clack-shhh. Clack-shhh.*

Lety did not speak English. Patrick's Spanish arrived in shy, bruised pieces, assembled from a phrasebook.

But they traded in a different language. Pigment for yarn. Stories for silence.

One evening, Lety motioned for him to come up to the roof.

She showed him the prickly pear cactus pads drying in the sun. They were covered in a white fungus.

"It is not a fungus," Lety said. She plucked one off. It was a tiny insect. A beetle.

She crushed it between her thumb and forefinger.

A smear of brilliant, violent red exploded onto her skin.

"Cochineal," she said. "The blood of the cactus."

Patrick stared at the colour. It was the red of cardinals. It was the red of spilled wine. It was the red of the birds he had painted taking flight from a bicycle wheel in New York.

"Teach me," Patrick said.

They spent the night grinding the dried beetles in the moonlight. Lety showed him how to mix the powder with lime juice to shift the hue toward coral, or with baking soda to push it toward purple.

Patrick took a small wooden panel. He dipped his brush into the beetle's blood.

He painted a London bus. He painted a red telephone box.

Then, he painted a scarf. A long woollen scarf, unspooled.

He knew the scarf Harold had given him was grey. But here, in the dust of Oaxaca, he painted it red. He let the cochineal transform the memory, turning the grey of mourning into something alive, something that bled.

He painted these exiled objects in a landscape of cactus and dust. He painted the red thread of his history stretching across the desert.

Lety watched him. She took the panel when it was dry. She hung it above her loom.

"So, the thread remembers," she said in Spanish. "It remembers what it was before it was woven."

He travelled south to Chiapas.

The mountains folded and unfolded like crumpled paper, green and mist shrouded. In San Cristóbal de las Casas, the air was thin and smelled of pine resin and woodsmoke.

He joined a collective of muralists. They were painting the walls of a community kitchen.

"Grab a brush, blondie!" the leader shouted, a man named Marco.

Patrick spent a week on scaffolding. They rendered Zapatista dolls with unblinking eyes and fists full of marigolds. They painted cornstalks that grew into stars.

They worked from dawn until the afternoon rain arrived. The rain in Chiapas was sudden and impartial. It washed the streets, turning the wet paint dripping onto the cobblestones into rivers of pink and green.

Children chased the rivulets, laughing, splashing in the colours. Their bare feet printed pale little ghosts onto the wet stones.

Patrick watched them. He felt a bubble rise in his chest.

He laughed.

It was a rusty sound. He had not laughed—truly laughed—since the funeral. The sound surprised him. It felt as if someone else had borrowed his throat for a moment.

Guatemala followed.

Lake Atitlán was a mirror ringed by volcanoes that kept their own counsel. The water was deep, holding secrets.

He stayed in a bamboo hut without electricity. He brushed his teeth with water drawn from a bucket that reflected stars the size of coins.

He painted by candlelight. The paper warped with the heat. The colours arrived on the page more vividly than he remembered mixing them, as if the candlelight were baking them into existence.

One morning, he woke to a vibration. *Zzzzummm.*

A hummingbird was trapped inside his mosquito net. It was battering the air, a blur of emerald and ruby, frantic.

Patrick sat up slowly. He opened the net.

"Go," he whispered.

The bird shot out. It vanished into the jungle.

Patrick felt the same release inside his ribs. Something bright and frantic that had been trapped in his chest since London darted outward. It left an ache, but it also left space.

Colombia. Bogotá at 2,600 metres.

The sky was close enough to bruise your knuckles on. Patrick climbed Monserrate at dawn, his lungs burning in the thin air.

He looked down at the waking city. A carpet of electric orange buses moving through the grey grid. The Andes standing guard like older brothers who had never learned to soften.

A street vendor sold him *agua de panela*: hot sugarcane water with lime.

It tasted like childhood cough syrup. It tasted like comfort.

"It is quite sweet," Patrick said.

The vendor, an old woman wrapped in a woollen ruana, nodded.

"That is the secret, my son: to endure, one needs a little more sweetness than they believe they deserve."

Patrick drank it all. He wrote the phrase in the margin of his sketch. He underlined it three times.

By the time the grant money dwindled to loose change, he had been away eighteen months.

He had filled four sketchbooks. He had posted twenty canvases back to Elena in Manhattan in cardboard tubes. He had traded so many small portraits for meals that his signature had simplified itself. He was no longer Patrick Evans. He was just a gesture. A loop. A mark.

He crossed the equator on a bus in Ecuador. The speedometer was broken, the needle resting on zero as they hurtled around the cliffs. The radio played only boleros.

In the border town of Ipiales, he hiked down the gorge to the Las Lajas Sanctuary. It was a gothic basilica wedged between the canyon walls, suspended over the river like a hand cupped around a candle.

He went inside. The air was thick with wax and whispers. Votive candles flickered in red glass cups.

He lit a candle.

"For Dad," he whispered.

He lit another.

"For the boy I was."

He lit a third. The flame wavered, then held tall.

"For Harold."

He watched them burn. He did not pray. He simply watched the light connect them.

He flew back to New York from Quito in late 2002.

He had three extra suitcases. They were overweight, stuffed with canvases that still smelled of woodsmoke, copal incense, and diesel.

Customs raised an eyebrow at the sheer volume of luggage.

Patrick paid the excess fee. He handed over the credit card Elena had sent him for emergencies. He felt the lightness that arrives when money is exchanged for something you cannot bear to leave behind.

Elena met him at JFK. She wore a trench coat, looking impervious to the chaos of the arrivals hall.

She saw him. Her eyes widened. She held out her arms.

"My God," she said. "You brought the entire horizon home."

Patrick hugged her. He laughed, and the sound was deeper, resonant, anchored in his chest.

Back at the warehouse studio in Chelsea, he unpacked.

He leaned the paintings against the raw brick walls. The room filled with colour. The turquoise of Taos. The indigo of Oaxaca. The bruised plum of the Andes.

The room looked like a continent cracked open.

Nek arrived an hour later. She brought tamales from a place in Queens and a bottle of mezcal.

They stood in the middle of the floor, turning in circles, letting the colours lap at their ankles.

Nek stopped in front of the Oaxaca canvas: the one with the red scarf dissolving into the dust.

She held it up to the light.

"You're not looking for him anymore," Nek said softly.

"Who?"

"The ghost. You stopped chasing him in the paint. You learned to let the place paint itself."

Patrick looked at the canvas. She was right. The red was no longer a wound. It was just a colour. It was just part of the landscape.

"I suppose I did," he said.

He felt the approval settle inside him like warm coins in a pocket.

That night, he slept on a futon in the studio.

The windows were open to the river of the city's sound. Sirens drifted up from Avenue C, mingling with the softer *clack-clack* of the freight elevator in the shaft.

He dreamed.

He dreamed of beetles drying on rooftops. He dreamed of a scar across volcanic stone. He dreamed of a red thread leaping an ocean, pulsing with current, but slack now: no longer pulling him, just connecting him.

When he woke, the warehouse was quiet. The paintings watched him like companions who had travelled a long way and were content, for now, to stand guard.

He made coffee on a hotplate.

He sat at his worktable. He opened the Winsor & Newton tin Harold had given him years before.

The half-pans were mostly empty. Only crusts of colour remained.

He wet his brush. He used the last stroke of cochineal red—the pigment he had ground with Lety—to paint a tiny image in the margin of a fresh, clean sketchbook.

A London bus.

Beneath it, he wrote the date: *December 2002.*

He wrote the city: *New York.*

And he wrote one word: *Return.*

The paint dried quickly in the winter heat of the studio, sealing the promise like a wax stamp on a letter he had not yet addressed, but finally, after all these miles, knew how to write.

Chapter VIII

Echoes of Home

October of 2005 arrived with skies the colour of tarnished pewter. The wind rattling the single-pane windows of the lecture hall smelled of coal smoke, damp wool, and early frost.

Patrick stood at the lectern, halfway through a morning lecture on Color Field painting. He was thirty-two years old now, wearing a corduroy jacket that had seen better days, trying to explain Rothko to a room of nineteen-year-olds who were almost entirely hungover, their faces pale beneath the fluorescent lights.

"The tragedy in Rothko," Patrick said, clicking the slide remote, "is not in the black. It is in the red. It is the vibration of a heart that is trying to stop beating."

The slide projector clicked. *Click-whir.* A massive rust-red rectangle filled the screen behind him, vibrating with projected light.

His mobile phone buzzed against the wood of the podium.

He usually ignored it. But the buzzing was persistent, frantic, like an insect trapped beneath a glass. He looked down. It was the Ealing landline.

He answered it, apologizing to the room with a raised hand.

"Hello?"

The voice was not his mother's. It was Mrs. Gable, the neighbour from number 42. Her voice was thin as onion skin, transparent with panic.

"Patrick? Is that you, dear?"

"I am here, Mrs. Gable."

"It's your mum, Patrick. I went in to check on her... she didn't answer the door. The ambulance is here, but..." The voice fractured, breaking into static. "She's gone, dear. She just... went. Peaceful. Like a candle going out."

Patrick stared at the Rothko slide. He looked at the rust-red rectangle. He waited for it to rearrange itself into something he could understand. A door. A window. An exit.

It did not. It remained only paint on canvas.

"Thank you, Mrs. Gable," Patrick said. His voice sounded as if it were coming from a radio in the next room, tinny and distant. "I will be there tonight."

He hung up. He looked at the students. They were watching him, pens poised, waiting for the rest of the sentence about Rothko.

"Class dismissed," Patrick said.

He walked out of the lecture hall. He stepped into the corridor, pressed his forehead against the cool concrete wall, and waited until the trembling stopped.

By evening, he was on a flight to Heathrow.

The cabin lights were dimmed to a pharmaceutical glow: that same sickly apricot hue he remembered from seven years ago.

He kept waiting for tears. He tried to summon them. He thought of his mother's lavender hedge. He thought of her hands, floured from baking, dusting the counter like snow.

But instead of tears, his body felt like a canvas left out in the rain: sodden, heavy, the image beneath already blurring into a grey pulp.

He watched the Atlantic unspool beneath the wing. It was a black page scattered with white ships like stars. He thought of the paper boat he had once set sailing in the Washington Square fountain, the one on which he had written *I am painting myself into existence*.

That boat had dissolved. This one was landing.

Heathrow at dawn smelled of industrial disinfectant and burnt toast. The car rental clerk handed him the keys to a Vauxhall Astra with the same practised courtesy Patrick remembered from graduation, from his father's funeral, from every return he had never wanted to make.

"Here for business or pleasure, sir?"

"Neither," Patrick said.

He drove toward the M4. It was already thick with white delivery vans, a river of commerce flowing into the city. He joined its slow crawl. He cracked the window, letting the winter air prickle his cheek.

Every junction announced itself like a line of dialogue from a half-forgotten play. Slough. Maidenhead. The exit for Windsor, where he and Harold had once skipped school to eat ice cream by the river, terrified and thrilled by their own rebellion.

He kept both hands on the steering wheel. He did not take the exit.

Ealing seemed smaller.

It looked as though someone had left the suburb in a pocket and forgotten to iron out the creases. The trees seemed lower. The distances seemed shorter.

The house on St. Albans Avenue was exactly as he had left it. The same cracked chimney. The same lavender hedge, now brown and brittle, bowing under the weight of the frost.

Only the front step had changed. Someone—a handyman, surely, not his mother—had painted it a cautious, sensible navy-blue.

Patrick stood on the pavement. He did not have to ring the bell. He had the key.

But he hesitated. He waited for the door to open. He waited for his mother to appear, her arms thin but certain, her eyes the same cornflower blue he remembered from every childhood fever. "Eat something green, darling."

The door remained closed.

He unlocked it. The mechanism was stiff.

Inside, the silence was absolute. It was not the silence of an empty house; it was the silence of a house that had stopped breathing.

The rooms felt curated rather than inhabited. His father's armchair still wore a lace antimacassar, pristine and white. The pipe rack was empty, but the scent of Balkan tobacco lingered in the curtains, a ghost refusing eviction.

On the sideboard sat a framed photograph. Patrick at nine years old. Gap-toothed. Holding a cardboard spaceship that was mostly sticky tape and hope.

Harold was just out of frame, but Patrick knew he was there. Harold had engineered the wings.

The edges of the photo were soft from handling. His mother must have held it often.

Patrick picked it up. He looked at the boy. He placed it face down. Then, feeling a wave of hot shame, he stood it upright again.

"I'm home, Mum," he whispered to the empty room.

The radiator clinked in response.

The next two days passed in the silence that follows a slammed door.

The neighbours arrived with casseroles. Mrs. Gable brought a lasagne that weighed as much as a small child. The kettle sang continually, boiling water for tea that no one truly drank.

Patrick answered questions on autopilot.

"Yes, the flight was fine."

"No, I am not teaching this term. I am on sabbatical."

"Yes, it was very sudden."

He slept in his old bedroom. It was an office now. A futon sat where the train set used to be. A computer monitor stared blankly from the desk where he used to draw lunar cities.

At night, he listened to the house settle. *Creak. Groan.*

It was the same creak he and Harold had once mistaken for burglars when they were ten. It was the same gurgle in the plumbing that sounded like distant laughter.

He lay on his back, staring at the ceiling. He waited for the grief to hit him. He wanted the crater. He wanted the explosion.

But the tears remained stubbornly out of reach. It felt as though grief were a colour he had forgotten how to mix. He had the tubes—loss, shock, memory—but he could not find the binder to make them stick.

The funeral was set for Wednesday.

Patrick chose the hymns. *Jerusalem. The Lord is my Shepherd.*

He signed the paperwork with the undertaker, whose suit whispered when he moved.

"Would you like to speak, sir?" the vicar asked.

Patrick nodded.

"Yes."

He wrote the eulogy at his mother's kitchen table at 3:00 a.m. The biro dug into the Formica. He wrote sentences and crossed them out. He struck through adjectives until only the barest bones remained.

She was kind. She liked lavender. She left the light on.

He finished with a line his father had once used to sign off letters, a phrase that made no sense yet meant everything: "We shall be glad of the rain when the lawn recovers."

He was not sure what it meant. But it sounded like forgiveness.

On the morning of the service, the sky delivered its own condolence.

Low, steady rain. It softened the edges of the headstones and turned the graveyard into a watercolour painting, blurring the line between earth and sky.

The church smelled of wet wool, damp stone, and chrysanthemums.

Patrick stood at the door. He shook hands he had not shaken since childhood. He accepted condolences from people who remembered him primarily as "the Evans boy who could draw."

"I am so sorry, Patrick."

"She was a saint, Patrick."

He moved through the nave. He saw faces from the past. Teachers. Neighbours.

Then he saw her. Carole. Her hair was now threaded with silver, cut into a sensible bob.

And beside her...

A navy-blue overcoat. Frayed at the cuff.

Harold.

He had arrived late. He was sitting at the back, near the baptismal font. His head was bowed. He was staring at the order of service as if it were a legal contract that might contain a loophole, a clause that could reverse the event.

He looked broader. Solid. An anchor disguised as a man.

Patrick felt his heart give a single, painful strike against his ribs. *He is here.*

They did not speak until the burial was over.

The earth hit the coffin like a slow, muffled applause. *Thump. Thump.*

The mourners drifted away toward the wake.

Patrick stood beside the fresh mound. The rain spattered his black coat.

He heard footsteps on the wet grass. He did not turn around.

"I wasn't sure if I should come," Harold said.

His voice was deeper, rougher than Patrick remembered.

Patrick turned. Harold was holding an umbrella, but it was closed. His hair was plastered to his skull. The rain ran down his face.

"I am glad you did," Patrick replied. And he meant it. He meant it more than anything he had said in years.

"How are you holding up?" Harold asked.

"I am not holding up," Patrick said. "I am just standing. There is a difference."

Harold nodded.

"Yes. There is."

They walked the long way back to the house.

They passed through the park. The stream was high, swollen by the rain. Frost had begun to lace the puddles on the path. Their footsteps shattered the thin ice. *Crack. Crack.*

Harold talked. He filled the silence with safe, rectangular topics.

"The firm moved again," Harold said. "Canary Wharf now. It's all glass. You would hate it. No shadows."

"And Sarah?" Patrick asked.

"She is ten. She is... formidable. She gave up the drums. Now she wants to be an architect. God help her."

Patrick smiled.

"It runs in the blood."

"Perhaps."

Harold looked at the river.

"The Thames still smells of rust when the tide goes out. I still hate it."

Patrick answered in monosyllables. His concentration was swallowed by the simple, overwhelming fact of having Harold by his side. The swing of their arms caused them to brush occasionally. Wool against wool. The friction created a small, necessary heat.

When they reached the junction where childhood had always bifurcated—where they had once parted ways a thousand times—Patrick stopped.

He looked at the street sign. Culvert Avenue.

"I keep thinking I should feel something larger," Patrick said, echoing the words he had spoken seven years ago. "I thought losing them both would be... a crater. But it is just a silence. It is just a lack of noise."

Harold turned to him. He was wearing leather gloves.

He reached out. He took Patrick's bare hand. He threaded their fingers together without ceremony.

"Do you remember what I told you?" Harold asked. "About the room?"

"That grief is a room you walk into," Patrick said. "And sometimes the switch doesn't work."

"I was wrong," Harold said softly.

Patrick looked at him.

"What?"

"It isn't a room, Pat. It's the whole house. You have to live in it. You must sleep in the bed and cook in the kitchen and sit in the chair, even when it is dark. Especially when it is dark."

The metaphor landed softly. It was an amendment. A correction to the blueprint.

Patrick squeezed Harold's hand. Once. Hard.

"I don't want to live in the dark," Patrick whispered.

"You won't," Harold said. "I will bring a torch."

They reached the door of the empty house.

Patrick fished the key from his pocket. It felt cold, foreign.

"Do you want to come in?" Patrick asked. "Mum has... well, there are no casseroles left. But there is whisky. Dad's old stuff."

Harold looked at the house. He looked at the dark windows.

"I have to pick Sarah up from school," Harold said. "Traffic."

Patrick felt a sharp pang of disappointment, quick and childish.

"Right," Patrick said. "Of course."

"But," Harold said. He turned back. He dug into the deep pocket of his overcoat.

"I didn't bring paints this time," Harold said. "You have enough paints."

He pulled out a small, rectangular box. It was wrapped in tissue paper.

Patrick took it.

He opened it.

Inside lay a fountain pen. It was vintage. The barrel was a deep, swirling green celluloid. The nib was gold.

"Green," Patrick whispered.

"Like the reeds," Harold said. "Like the quills dipped in ink. Do you remember?"

Patrick looked up. His vision blurred.

"For planning," Harold said. "You cannot simply paint the world, Patrick. Sometimes you must write it. You must plan the city before you build it."

Patrick closed his hand around the pen. It was warm from Harold's pocket.

"Thank you," Patrick said, his voice strangled.

Then, because the day had already broken all the rules, because they were orphans of the same history, Patrick leaned forward.

He kissed Harold's cheek.

It was quick. Dry. The scratch of cold skin and the taste of rain.

Harold did not move.

But his eyes closed. For the duration of a heartbeat, perhaps two, he stayed there, receiving the touch.

When he stepped back, the space between them felt altered. It was not empty. It was charged. An invisible thread, which had been slack for years, had pulled taut once again.

"I will call you," Harold said. "Tomorrow."

"Tomorrow," Patrick repeated.

Harold turned around. He walked away.

Patrick watched the navy-blue overcoat walk away, turn the corner, and vanish into the grey afternoon.

Only then did he go inside.

The house smelled of lilies and stale perfume. It was quiet.

Patrick climbed the stairs to his old bedroom. He sat at the desk.

He placed the green fountain pen on the wood.

Outside, the rain eased into mist. Somewhere, a siren doppler away. Somewhere, a dog barked.

Patrick picked up the pen. He uncapped it. The gold nib gleamed.

He opened a notebook.

He wrote the date. October 2005.

He wrote: *The light switch is broken.*

Then, beneath it, he wrote: *But I am not in the dark.*

He sat there for a long time, listening to the house settle around him, dreaming of footsteps shattering the frost, of a scarf that smelled of cedar, and of a future that was finally, terrifyingly, blank enough to begin.

Chapter IX

Almost Seen

The day after the funeral, Patrick walked around Ealing in circles.

He wore his black overcoat with the collar turned up against the wind. His shoes still carried a faint dusting of graveyard dirt on the welt, a lingering, gritty reminder of the earth hitting the oak.

He had told Mrs. Gable, who insisted on hovering over him in the kitchen, that he needed air. That he would buy milk. That perhaps he would look at his grandmother's old house on the other side of the borough.

Mrs. Gable had nodded, understanding the codes of grief: the need to stay in motion to keep the thoughts from settling. She had pressed a ten-pound note into his palm, a reflex from a time when he was twelve years old and ten pounds was a fortune.

"Buy yourself something sweet, darling," she had whispered.

Patrick walked. The ten-pound note grew warm and damp in his fist.

At the corner of Culvert Avenue, he stopped in front of the shuttered video rental shop. It used to be a Blockbuster. Now it was an empty shell. A new poster in the window advertised broadband internet. The familiar plastic letters that once spelled out "New Releases" and "Betamax" had been replaced by a blinking neon sign. OPEN... CLOSED... OPEN...

Nothing stays still long enough to mourn it, he thought. *Except people. People stay still in memory for a long time, refusing to be renovated.*

He took the number 65 bus out of habit. He climbed the narrow, twisting stairs to the top deck and sat in the front seat—the "driver's seat"—where he and Harold used to sit, dangling their legs and pretending to steer the massive vehicle through the traffic.

The route had changed. There were new roundabouts with municipal flowerbeds that looked too symmetrical to be real. But the railway bridge still wore the same soot-stained smile, the brickwork dyed by decades of diesel fumes.

He got off at the stop before the park. He let his feet carry him, bypassing his conscious brain, toward the high street.

Ken's Family Grocer was gone. In its place stood a shiny chain convenience store with a blue plastic awning and fluorescent lighting that hummed like a headache.

Patrick went inside. The aisles had been widened. The chaotic shelves of his childhood—stacked with dusty tins and penny sweets—had vanished, replaced by orderly rows of products with prices printed on stickers.

He bought a carton of milk he didn't need. He queued behind a young mother whose toddler was sitting in the trolley seat, repeatedly dropping a plastic tractor onto the linoleum floor. *Bang.*

The mother sighed, picking it up. *Bang.*

The boy looked at Patrick. He had eyed the exact, warm brown of Harold's.

Patrick's breath caught. He looked away, paid quickly with the ten-pound note, and left without taking his change.

Outside, the rain began.

It was a soft, deliberate drizzle that darkened the pavement in spots like a developing photograph.

Patrick turned up his collar. He walked past the estate agent, where the photos of houses smiled like people who had already decided you couldn't afford them.

He found himself standing outside Number 42.

Harold's house.

Or, the house Harold had grown up in.

A *For Sale* sign stood in the front garden, leaning slightly to the left. The front door, which Harold's father had once painted a defiant scarlet, was now a cautious, council-approved grey.

Patrick stopped. He pressed his palm against the cold iron of the gate. He pushed.

Click.

The latch made the same sound it always had. A small, mechanical sound that opened a much larger room inside him.

He walked up the path. He expected to feel like an intruder, but the concrete welcomed his stride. The privet hedge had been trimmed into a polite cube. The apple tree at the back—the one they had climbed to look for the horizon—was gone. He could see the gap in the fence where it used to be.

He remembered climbing it at twelve years old. Harold had stood below, shouting instructions on weight distribution. "Don't put your foot there, Pat, the branch is compromised." They had both been convinced that the view from the top would show them a map of the future.

It hadn't. It had only shown them more roofs, more chimneys, and the same indifferent sky.

Patrick stood on the threshold. He wasn't going to knock. He just wanted to stand there.

Then the door opened.

A woman stood there. She was in workout gear, her ponytail high and tight. Earbuds hung around her neck like extra limbs. She smiled with the neutral, guarded smile of modern city living.

"Are you looking for someone?" she asked.

Patrick took a step back, flustered.

"I'm sorry. I... used to live nearby. I was just reminiscing."

She softened instantly. She mistook his grief-stricken expression for simple nostalgia.

"Oh! We only moved in last year," she said, pulling an earbud out completely. "Did the previous owner pass away? Old Mr. Carrington? Lovely man. Incredibly quiet."

Patrick felt a pang. Harold's father was gone too. The generation was being erased.

"Yes," Patrick said. "He was."

"He left a box of things in the loft," the woman said. "We've been meaning to clear it out. You're welcome to have a look if you'd like. Before it goes to the tip."

Patrick should have declined. He should have walked away.

But curiosity spoke for him before caution could intervene.

"Just a quick look," he said.

He followed her inside.

The house smelled different. It smelled of coffee pods and citrus cleaner, not the scent of lavender and old paper of the Carringtons.

But the staircase still creaked on the third step. Patrick stepped over it instinctively.

The woman pointed to the loft hatch.

"The ladder's down. Help yourself. I'll be in the kitchen."

Patrick climbed into the dark.

The loft smelled of dust and insulation. A single bare bulb illuminated a stack of cardboard boxes.

He lifted the first lid.

School exercise books. The rubber bands holding them together had perished into red dust.

He opened a blue book. Geography.

Inside was Harold's childhood handwriting. Cramped. Slanted. Urgent.

Even at ten years old, Harold wrote as if he were drafting a treaty.

The Amazon rainforest is the lungs of the world. Without it, we cannot breathe.

Patrick turned the page. A loose scrap of paper fell out.

It was a note, written in pencil that had almost vanished, the graphite shining faintly.

Meet me at the oak tree when the moon rises.

Patrick's pulse stumbled. He touched the paper. He closed the book quickly, as if to trap the words before they escaped into the freezing air of the loft.

He dug deeper. Beneath the books lay a photograph.

He pulled it out.

It was the two of them. Fourteen years old. Standing in Pitshanger Park.

They had their arms thrown over each other's shoulders. Their mouths were open in laughter: that unguarded, ugly, beautiful laughter of boys who have not yet learned to hide.

The print had faded to the soft blues of old denim and cyan. But the joy was intact. It was a small animal, still breathing inside the frame.

Patrick turned it over.

On the back, in Harold's careful script:

Patrick and me. Pitshanger Park, 1987. The day we saw the heron.

Patrick remembered. He remembered the bird rising from the stream. He remembered the shared gasp. He remembered the way Harold's hand had found his shoulder and stayed there, heavy, and warm, long after the bird had vanished.

Footsteps on the ladder.

The woman's head appeared.

"Find anything useful?"

Patrick slipped the photograph and the geography book into the deep pocket of his overcoat.

"Just memories," he said, his voice thick. "May I keep these?"

She waved a hand.

"Take the lot if you want. We're clearing out. Baby on the way."

"Congratulations," Patrick said.

"Thanks. Just... shut the hatch when you're done."

Patrick climbed down the stairs. He carried only the photo and the book. At the door, he thanked her. He offered to post anything else to the estate, but she was already adjusting her earbuds, already jogging on the spot.

"No need," she said. "They're just things."

Outside, the rain had thickened to a steady drum. *Drum-drum-drum.*

Patrick walked without direction. He passed through the park gates. He walked past the bench where they had once shared a bag of crisps and sworn eternal allegiance to the idea of "Another Place."

The bench was new. Pale treated wooden slats that had never known their sixteen-year-old weight.

He sat down anyway. The rain spotted the milk carton in his plastic carrier bag.

He pulled out the photograph.

The water beaded on the surface. He wiped it gently with his sleeve.

The day we saw the heron.

A bus pulled up to the stop opposite. The brakes sighed. *Hiss.*

It was the same route number they had ridden home after their first trip to the cinema. Ghostbusters. Pear drops. The shared armrest sticky with sugar. The moment their elbows touched and neither moved.

The bus doors opened. No one got off. The doors closed. The bus carried on.

Patrick remained where he was. He held the photo between his index finger and thumb. His heart performed a slow, deliberate strike against his ribs.

He thought about sending a text message.

He pulled out his phone.

I found something of ours.

He looked at the screen. The words felt too small. They felt too small for the weather, for the years, for the death of their parents, for the way the hedge at Number 42 had been clipped into a shape that no longer recognized them.

He deleted the message.

He slipped the photo inside his coat, next to his heart. He stood up.

The walk home took longer.

The rain softened every edge of Ealing. It turned the streetlamps into watercolour halos of orange and white.

At his parents' door—his door, now—he stopped. He looked back down the street.

No one was following him. Nothing was shouting his name.

Yet the air felt electric. It felt as if the city had inhaled and forgotten to exhale.

He pressed a palm against the pocket where the photograph waited. He felt the faint hum of the paper against his bone.

He went inside.

The house was warm. Mrs. Gable had left the heating on. She had left a note on the table: *"Gone to Bingo. Left a Cottage Pie in the oven for you. Eat it."*

Patrick smiled. He took off his wet coat.

He placed the photo on the kitchen table.

He sat down. He stared at it.

He remembered something Mrs. Gable had told him two days ago, in the blur of the wake. He hadn't processed it then, but it surfaced now.

"He called once, you know," Mrs. Gable had said, pouring tea. "Your friend. The tall one. Harold."

"When?" Patrick had asked, distracted.

"Oh, years ago. A year or so after you went to New York. He called your mum. Asked how you were."

Patrick sat up straighter in the empty kitchen.

"What did Mum say?"

"She told him you were painting. That you were happy. He said... he said he didn't want to disrupt your momentum. Didn't leave a number."

Patrick's throat closed.

Momentum.

It was exactly the word Harold would use. A word from physics. Mass times velocity.

Harold had not abandoned him. Harold had taken a step back to let him fly. Safety before identity. Harold had calculated the trajectory and realized that his gravity might pull Patrick back to earth too soon.

So, he had stayed silent.

"Idiot," Patrick whispered to the empty room. "Noble idiot."

Outside, the rain eased into a mist that blurred every boundary between the garden and the sky.

Patrick carried the photograph upstairs.

He placed it on the windowsill of his bedroom.

Beside it lay the green fountain pen. And the old tin of watercolours.

The three objects—paper, plastic, metal—seemed to recognize one another. Like old friends meeting in a foreign railway station.

Patrick opened the tin.

He picked up a brush. He wet the half-pan of cochineal red—the pigment from Mexico—coaxing the last ghost of colour from the dry crust with a drop of rainwater he gathered from the windowpane.

He painted.

He painted a tiny red London bus in the corner of the photograph's white border.

It felt absurd. It felt necessary. It was a promise to keep moving, even when the route had changed.

He took a breath.

He picked up his phone.

He didn't think. He didn't let caution intervene. He didn't let the years weigh down his hand.

He typed:

I found something of ours. I thought you might like it back.

He took a photo of the image with the little painted bus.

His thumb hovered over the button.

Send.

The message shot away.

He placed the phone face down on the windowsill.

He sat there, staring at the window until the glass darkened and his own reflection appeared: older, paint-stained, tired, but waiting.

And behind his reflection, the night stretched wide open. It was patient. It was not afraid.

Chapter X

The Weight of Expectations

Harold Carrington entered the world in 1973, in the same hospital ward as Patrick Evans, three weeks later and two beds away. Neither of them would know this fact until university records accidentally revealed it decades later.

He was the third child that Arthur and Margaret Carrington hoped would be their last. He was born into a house already organized around unyielding routines: his father's silent toast at half past six, the snap of briefcase latches at seven, his mother's ledger open on the kitchen table at eight.

From the beginning, Harold was the final brushstroke on a meticulously planned canvas. He was small, measured, and necessary to balance the composition.

Arthur Carrington worked for the Ealing borough planning office. He was a man who measured streets the way other men measured time: with heavy plastic set squares, with topographical maps folded like sacred texts, and with a deep, abiding suspicion of anything that was not parallel. He spoke little, but when he did, the words arrived fully formed, polished, and dense, as if council approval had been sought and granted before he opened his mouth.

Harold learned early to stand beside his father's drafting table. He watched the streets of London take shape beneath the pencil's graphite. He understood, before he could read, that straight lines were moral and curves required justification.

"Structure, Harold. Structure stops the roof from falling on your head. Decoration is what people use to hide bad engineering."

Margaret Carrington balanced budgets for the local authority. Numbers marched across her page like well-drilled soldiers, column after column of black ink. At home, she applied the same rigour to the household accounts. There was a column for milk, a column for school shoes, and, Harold suspected, a column for virtue.

She loved her son with the precision she applied to her ledgers. She rationed praise the way wartime cooks rationed eggs: enough to bind the mixture, but never enough to make it rise.

"That is adequate, Harold," she would say when he brought home an A. "Consistent."

Consistency was the family religion. They lived in a terraced house on a road where all the houses had been built in the same year, 1935, and painted within the same three shades of beige. Harold's bedroom overlooked the back gardens, a view of wooden fences so identical they could have been printed on a single sheet of wallpaper and pasted over the window.

At night, Harold listened to the house. The central heating timer clicked. *Click*. The pipes sighed. *Wheeze*. It was the sound of a life that had been pre-approved, costed to the final penny, and insured against acts of God or outbursts of passion.

At five years old, he followed his sisters to St. Benedict's.

The sleeves of his blazer already reached his knuckles. His shoes were polished to a shine in which you could read disappointment.

The playground was a chaos of elbows, scraped knees, and vowels that stretched like chewing gum. Harold moved through it with the deliberate calm of a boy who had been taught that noise was inefficient. He stood near the wall, observing the structural integrity of the play area.

He shared a classroom with a boy named Patrick Evans.

Patrick was a blur. Patrick was untucked shirts and gravity-defying hair. Patrick was a boy who dropped things and laughed about it.

During the first year, they barely spoke. They were two planets orbiting the same sun at different speeds, destined never to collide.

Friendship arrived sideways, the way change always did in Harold's life.

It was a Tuesday. Raining.

They both reached for the same library book on the bottom shelf. *The Usborne Book of Space Exploration*.

Harold's hand touched the spine. Patrick's hand touched Harold's.

Static electricity flared between them. A tiny, audible snap.

Patrick snatched his hand back, his eyes wide.

"Did you feel that?"

"Static electricity," Harold said automatically. "The carpet."

"It's a sign," Patrick corrected. He pulled the book out. He opened it to a page showing the rings of Saturn. "Look. I am going there."

Harold looked at the illustration.

"You can't. The gas pressure would crush a human."

Patrick looked at him. He didn't mock him. He simply smiled.

"Not if we build the ship properly. You build it. I'll fly it."

After that, gravity shifted. Harold slipped into Patrick's orbit the way a moon slips into a tide: powerlessly, inevitably.

He liked the way Patrick saw shapes in the clouds where Harold only saw cumulus formations. He liked the way Patrick could turn a cardboard box into a spaceship with just two cuts and a strip of sticky tape.

Harold provided the ballast. When Patrick wanted to climb the oak tree, Harold checked the branches for rot. When Patrick wanted to mix "Martian dust," Harold found the red brick dust in the garage.

At home, Harold said little about the new friendship. The Carringtons did not deal in anecdotes.

When Patrick's name appeared on a birthday list, Arthur Carrington nodded once. He filed the information under "Social Development, Age Appropriate."

"Do the Evans family keep a clean kitchen?" Margaret Carrington asked.

"Yes," Harold lied.

He had never seen their kitchen. He had only seen their garden, where the lavender grew so thick it hummed with bees, and where the grass was never short enough to please his father.

Adolescence arrived with its usual forged documents.

A cracking voice. Sudden, painful inches of height. The discovery that rules could be bent if you leaned on them hard enough.

Harold grew faster than his coordination could file the paperwork. He tripped over his own feet.

Football became a solution. It was a language he could speak without an accent. The pitch offered a geometry his father approved of lines, zones, tactics.

Harold learned to tackle with the same neat finality his mother applied to her month-end columns. He stopped the chaos. He intercepted the ball. He restored order.

"Economy of movement," his coach praised him.

Arthur repeated the phrase at dinner, carving his roast beef.

"Economy of movement. Good. Sport aligns with accounting, Harold. It is all about resource management."

Girls noticed the new economy, too.

Lucy Fenton, all copper hair and certainty, latched onto him during a geography field trip to the Lake District. Her fingers found his as if they had been pencilled into the timetable weeks ago.

Harold let them stay. He was curious. He was not displeased.

She tasted of green apple chewing gum and ambition. She spoke in exclamation marks. When she kissed him behind the science block, pressing him against the rough brick, Harold waited for the explosion.

He felt... warmth. He felt a mild, pleasant friction. It was the way a filing cabinet might feel if you rested your fingers against the sun-warmed metal.

Safe. Solid. Metal.

He told Patrick none of this.

At fifteen years old, they were sitting on opposite sides of the classroom. The aisle between them was a demilitarized zone. Neither had agreed to cross it, but the treaties had been signed in silence.

Patrick kept his head down. He drew heroes in his sketchbook whose capes were the exact shade of red as Harold's football shirt.

Harold kept his eyes on the pitch. On Lucy. On anything that did not ask him to name the ache that had begun knocking against his ribs like an unauthorized second heart.

The kiss at the leaving party arrived uninvited.

July of 1991. The end of Sixth Form.

The party was in someone's basement. It smelled of cheap cider, dry ice, and the sudden, terrifying realization that childhood had an exit door, and they were being pushed through it.

Harold was drunk. Not falling drunk but blurred. The edges of his straight lines were wavering.

He found Patrick in the boys' toilets.

Patrick was washing his hands. He looked pale. The fluorescent light hummed, green and sickly.

"Are you all right?" Harold asked. The door closed behind him, muffling the music.

"Too much noise," Patrick murmured. He looked at Harold in the mirror. "Are you going to university? Reading, right?"

"Yes. Education."

"Sensible."

"Someone has to be."

Patrick turned around. He leaned back against the sink.

"I am going to miss you, H. Even if you are a sensible idiot."

The air in the room thickened. It smelled of bleach and panic.

Harold took a step forward. He didn't plan it. It wasn't on the schedule.

He took Patrick's face in his hands. He held it the way you might hold a very fragile and incredibly old document you were afraid of creasing.

Patrick stopped breathing. His eyes widened.

Harold leaned in.

Their mouths met.

It was clumsy. It was urgent. It tasted of smoke, cider, and goodbye. It was not a pleasant warmth. It was a demolition. It was the sound of the roof falling in.

When it ended, Harold pulled away, panting. He felt the room tilt. He felt as if someone had adjusted the axis of the earth without consulting the planning department.

Patrick looked at him, his lips red, his eyes searching.

"Harold?"

Terror flooded Harold's chest. Cold, absolute terror.

This was a curve. This was a deviation. This was a structural failure.

"I am sorry," Harold said, his voice strangled. "Drunk. I'm sorry."

He walked away first. Because walking away was what Arthur Carrington's son did. Straight lines. No curves.

That night, he wrote the incident in his head like a report.

Anomaly observed: 23:00 hours. Cause: Alcohol/Stress. Action: File under Confidential. Seal. Forget.

He dated it. He sealed it. And he spent the next decade trying to lose the key.

University offered a geography of a different scale.

Thames Valley. Red brick corridors. The possibility of starting again, of rewriting the code.

Harold threw himself into conformity. He chose Education, a subject his father called "sensible lateral growth."

He dated girls who talked about lesson plans and wedding favours. Girls whose fathers asked about pension schemes during the Sunday roast.

He learned to say "mortgage" without flinching. He learned to nod when professors spoke of "appropriate boundaries."

He saw Patrick, of course. They had their coffee. They had their mornings in the launderette.

But every time Patrick looked at him—really looked at him—Harold saw the reflection in the bathroom mirror. He saw the panic. So, he held Patrick's wrist in the launderette, felt the pulse, and then let go. He let go because holding on meant falling, and Harold Carrington did not fall.

He met Eleanor in his second year.

She was kind. She was pragmatic. She liked spreadsheets.

She fit into his life the way a manila folder fits into a suspension file: snug, labelled, easy to retrieve.

They married at twenty-two in a registry office where the carpet was the same beige as his childhood hallway.

Arthur shook his hand afterward.

"Good trajectory, son. Solid match."

Margaret cried precisely one tear per cheek. Then she asked the caterer for an itemized receipt for the buffet.

Sarah arrived first. A loud, demanding miracle born in 1995. A boy followed two years later. Both born during the half-term holidays for maximum efficiency.

Harold learned to assemble flat-pack cots. He learned to read bedtime stories with voices that didn't waver. He learned to kiss Eleanor goodnight with the same measured tenderness he applied to his tax returns.

At dinner parties, he talked about Key Stages and interest rates. If anyone noticed his eyes drift toward the window when laughter erupted in a different octave outside, nobody mentioned it.

The years passed in orderly columns.

But you cannot engineer against damp.

The marriage developed hairline cracks. Small at first. Invisible to the untrained eye.

Eleanor felt his distance. She felt the way he held himself back, a fortress with the drawbridge permanently raised.

"Where do you go?" she asked him one night, watching him stare at the television without seeing it. "You are here, Harry. But you are not here."

"I am tired," Harold said. "It's the exams."

It wasn't the marking. It was the effort of holding up the roof when the foundations were missing.

The cracks widened. Even Eleanor's spreadsheets could not balance the deficit of affection.

They separated with the politeness of two civil servants dividing stationery.

"I think you need to figure out who you are," Eleanor said, handing him a box of books. She wasn't angry. She was just sad. "Because I don't think you ever introduced him to me."

Harold moved into a flat in Hammersmith.

The radiator clanked like a bad heart. The view offered only a brick wall, and a slice of sky so narrow it could have been pencilled into the margin.

He heard about Patrick's departure to New York. He heard it the way you hear about an earthquake in a distant country: headlines, no details.

Patrick Evans is gone.

Harold did not write. He filed the name under "Archived Correspondence." He told himself the folder was closed.

Folders spring open, however.

A Friday in late October 2005, after the funeral flowers had wilted and the condolence calls had ceased, Harold returned to his empty flat.

He was tired. His father was gone. His mother was gone. The old house on Culvert Avenue was sold.

He dropped his keys into the bowl.

His phone vibrated in his pocket.

He pulled it out. A text message.

I found something of ours. I thought you might like it back.

An image loaded.

It was a photo of the two of them. Pitshanger Park. 1987. Laughing.

And in the corner, a freshly painted little red bus.

Harold stared at the screen. The pixelated image burned into his retina.

He looked at the shelf by the window.

There, sitting in the dust, was the tin of watercolours Patrick had returned to him after his father's funeral years ago.

Harold picked it up. Twelve half-pans. Still bearing a fingerprint of cobalt blue.

He placed it on the windowsill. He told himself it was only pigment. Only metal. Only memory.

But memory has a way of bleeding into the present. The way cobalt can stain a white shirt no matter how many times you wash it.

Harold sat down at his small kitchen table.

He did not reply to the text message immediately.

Instead, he found a sheet of printer paper. He opened the tin. He went to the sink and filled a glass with water.

He began, without planning it, to paint.

Not for galleries. Not for Patrick. Only for the silence that fell when the brush met the paper.

He painted the view from his window. The brick wall. The narrow sky. The cage he had built for himself.

And then, dipping his brush into the red pan, he added a single line.

Thin as a hair. Somewhere in the composition. A red thread running through the brickwork, interrupting the mortar.

He told himself it was balance. He told himself it was composition.

He did not name it Thread. He did not name it Scarf. He did not name it Patrick.

But it stayed there. Patient as ink. Waiting for the day he would follow it out of the margin, pick up the phone, and finally, finally, step onto the open page.

Chapter XI

Digital Ghosts

Patrick's life in New York had settled into a rhythm of quiet, curated survival.

It was the spring of 2011. He was thirty-eight years old.

He woke before the alarm, usually at 5:30 a.m., when the rubbish lorries were still lumbering noisily down 23rd Street, chewing through the city's refuse. He drank black coffee from a ceramic mug he had thrown himself at a pottery studio in Santa Fe: a heavy, imperfect mug that held the heat longer than anything factory-made.

He painted until the light shifted from the bruised blue of dawn to the hard, unforgiving grey of mid-morning.

Then, he crossed the island.

He walked to the School of Visual Arts, where he taught a module on Memory and Materiality. The undergraduate students, children of the nineties who wore oversized headphones and ironic t-shirts, called him "Prof," or, occasionally, "Evans." They copied his London vowels, softening their hard American *R*s when they asked for extensions on their essays, hoping the accent would grant them mercy.

"It is about restraint," Patrick would tell them, circling a student's overly busy canvas with a paint-stained finger. "You do not have to shout to be heard. Sometimes a whisper breaks the glass."

The nights belonged to the warehouse studio in Chelsea. It smelled of turpentine, drying linseed oil, and the expensive cedar incense Nek burned to keep the rats away.

He had exhibitions in small, respectable galleries on the Lower East Side.

The reviews in *Artforum* used words like "restraint," "maturity," and "architectural melancholy."

He had a circle of friends—mostly other expats or gallery staff—who knew the rules. They knew you could ask Patrick about technique. You could ask him about colour theory. But you did not ask him why he never kept a painting once it dried. You did not ask him why his landscapes always felt as if they were waiting for someone who had just stepped out of the frame.

He told himself that the past was a room he had bricked up, leaving only a slit for air. It was safe. It was structural.

Then the group exhibition arrived in March.

It was titled *Intersect*. Elena, who now ran a larger space in SoHo, hung Patrick's largest piece on the main wall.

It was a canvas measuring six feet by four. An expanse of deep, velvety indigo: a London night, heavy with damp and the unspoken. Bisected down the centre was a single, violent line of red.

It was not just a line. It was a thread. Painted with a fine-hair brush using cochineal pigment, it coiled and frayed, leaping the gap of the dark. It was an open vein upon the canvas.

Opening night was unusually warm. The gallery doors were propped open, letting in the noise of Broadway. The room smelled of expensive white wine, new money, and the sharp, chemical taste of ambition.

Patrick stood near a pillar, holding a glass of sparkling water. He wore a charcoal grey suit that fit him like armour.

"It's very... visceral," a collector said, leaning in, his breath smelling of mints and Chardonnay. "Is it a wound?"

"It is a connection," Patrick said. "Or a knot. It depends on the light."

The students were there. They were armed with smartphones, filtering the world through glass screens.

A new application had been gaining traction that year. Instagram. Patrick did not understand it. It was a way of archiving the present before having even lived it.

He watched a girl with pink hair raise her mobile phone toward his painting. *Click*.

She typed rapidly.

#LondonNight #ArtThatRemembers #RedThread #SVA

She posted it.

Patrick watched her thumb press 'Share'. He felt a strange, prickling sensation on the back of his neck, a phantom touch. As if someone had just walked over his grave.

Within hours, the image was reposted. It was pinned on blogs. It was shared on Tumblr. It spread into the digital ether: tiny binary signals that seemed harmless, like pollen on the wind, but which carried the weight of history.

Three thousand miles away, in the common room of a dormitory in Massachusetts, the ripples hit the shore.

It was a boarding school just outside Boston. The room smelled of boys' deodorant, microwave popcorn, and the stale scent of adolescence.

Thomas Carrington was fourteen years old. He was gangly, with hair that refused to lie flat: a genetic inheritance from a father who believed in order but produced chaos. He should have been studying Algebra. Instead, he was scrolling.

His thumb swiped the screen upwards. Meme. Meme. Girl from physics class. Meme.

Then, the algorithm served him something else.

It was a suggested post. Art That Remembers.

Thomas stopped scrolling.

The thumbnail caught his eye. It was abstract, but it vibrated with something he recognized.

The indigo. The shape of the shadows. It looked like the view from the window of the house in Ealing where he had spent his early childhood before the divorce, before the move to America, before the silence settled in.

And the red line.

It looked exactly like the little red painted bus in the photograph his dad kept in the bottom drawer of his bedside table. The photograph Thomas had found once while looking for batteries, hidden beneath a stack of handkerchiefs.

Thomas tilted the screen.

Harold Carrington was sitting in the armchair in the corner of the common room. He was visiting for the weekend, reading a thick biography of Churchill, building a wall of words between himself and the world.

Harold had transferred to the Boston office of his law firm three years ago. He had wanted a clean slate. He had wanted distance from the damp ghosts of London.

"Dad," Thomas called out. "Look at this."

Harold lowered the book. He adjusted his glasses.

"What is it? Another silly video?"

"No. It's art. But look." Thomas walked over. He shoved the phone under Harold's nose. "It reminds me of that photo you have. The one with the painted bus."

Harold looked at the glowing rectangle.

His heart performed a forbidden flip in his chest. *Thump-flip.*

He took the phone. His hand trembled slightly.

He knew that brushstroke. He knew the way the indigo pooled into violet near the bottom, suggesting wet pavement and regret. He knew the specific, violent shade of red. It was the same red Patrick had used to paint the bus on the photo in 2005. It was the same red thread that Harold himself had painted in secret, alone in his Hammersmith flat, trying to stitch a life back together.

He knew it the way you know your own pulse when you wake at 3:00 a.m. and cannot remember why you are still alive.

"Who painted this?" Harold asked. His voice was remarkably quiet, stripped of its usual legal resonance.

Thomas took the phone back. He tapped the tag.

"It says here... 'Prof. P. Evans.' School of Visual Arts, New York."

Thomas tapped again. A profile loaded.

A thumbnail photograph.

It showed a man. Older. Hair peppered with grey at the temples. Wearing a charcoal grey suit. But the eyes were the same. Almost black. Holding the light as if it were a question he was waiting to answer.

Patrick.

Harold's throat filled with weather. It filled with rain and fog and the smell of lilac and wet wool.

"Dad?" Thomas asked. "Are you alright?"

Harold stood up. He closed the Churchill book.

"Yes," Harold said. "I used to know him. A long time ago."

He waited until Thomas went to his room.

Harold was staying in a guest suite on campus. The kitchen was sterile, lit by a buzzing fluorescent strip. *Mmmmmm.*

It reminded him of university launderettes. Of 5:00 a.m. coffees. Of the silence before the mistake.

He opened his laptop.

He typed the name slowly. P-a-t-r-i-c-k E-v-a-n-s.

He typed it as if the keys might bruise him if he struck them too hard.

The screen filled with results.

Patrick Evans: The Architecture of Absence. Review: Evans's New Exhibition Astounds. Faculty Page: SVA.

The screen offered a studio email address. A PO Box. Nothing personal. No telephone number. Only a digital void where a voice should be.

Harold opened his email client.

He stared at the blinking cursor. It pulsed like a heartbeat.

He drafted a message:

I saw your painting. It is magnificent. H.

He deleted it. Too cold.

The red thread... did you mean...?

He deleted it. Too needy.

I am sorry.

He stared at that one for a long time. *I am sorry I let go of your wrist. I am sorry I married Eleanor. I am sorry I was so afraid of the curve that I tried to live in a straight line until it strangled me.*

He deleted it. Not sorry enough.

He closed the draft.

Instead, he clicked into the gallery's online viewing room.

The painting rotated in a sterile white space. *London Night / Red Thread (2011).*

Beside it was a price tag. It was a number that would pay Harold's mortgage for three months.

He clicked Add to Cart.

He stared at the checkout screen. He wanted it. He wanted to own the evidence. He wanted to hang it on his wall and look at it every day and bleed.

Then, shame washed over him.

He could not buy this. You cannot buy a memory you helped to create. You cannot own what you have already lost.

He closed the browser window.

He poured himself a finger of whisky. He left it untouched on the counter, the amber liquid catching the fluorescent light.

He went over to his suitcase. He unzipped the side pocket.

He pulled out the photograph.

He had packed it. He always packed it. It travelled with him like a passport to a country that no longer existed.

It was the photo Patrick had sent him in 2005. Pitshanger Park. 1987. And in the corner, the little red bus painted with cochineal pigment.

He held it up to the bedside lamp. The red paint caught the light and gleamed.

Somewhere inside that image lived a night of frost and sparklers. Somewhere inside lived the smell of cedar and safety.

He told himself it was only paper. Only paint. Only memory.

But memory has a way of fraying when you need it to stay whole.

The next morning, he sent an email from work.

He sat in his office in the Prudential Tower, overlooking the Charles River. The office was all glass and steel, an aquarium for men in suits.

He chose a subject line as neutral as contract law.

Subject: Gallery Exhibition

He wrote:

Dear Patrick,

I saw your exhibition. Thomas found it. Congratulations. The red line is... striking.

If you ever find yourself north of Boston, I'll treat you to a coffee.

Harold Carrington

He signed it formally. As if addressing a colleague or a client. As if he had not once held Patrick's face in his hands in a basement that smelled of cider.

He kept the mouse hovering.

Click.

Sent.

He leaned back, his heart hammering against his ribs like a trapped bird.

The reply arrived three hours later.

Harold watched the notification appear. *From: P. Evans Studio.*

He opened it. It was short enough to read in a single breath.

Harold—

I am teaching at a summer residency in Provincetown all of July.

If you are free, the ferry arrives at noon on the 12th.

P.

Harold read the message twice. Then a third time.

He placed his palms flat on the mahogany desk. This desk had witnessed mergers. It had witnessed divorces. It had witnessed the small, neat signatures of a life organized into columns.

He closed the email.

He opened his physical diary: a leather-bound planner he kept because pixels felt too impermanent.

He picked up his fountain pen.

On the 12th of July, with the same steady handwriting that had once recorded exam results and wedding anniversaries, he wrote:

Ferry.

The ink dried quickly. It sealed what he had not yet decided to begin.

The weeks passed in orderly increments.

June melted into July. The heat in Boston swelled, baking the pavement, turning the city into a furnace.

Harold told no one where he was going. He told his secretary he needed a long weekend.

On the morning of the twelfth, he packed a small holdall. Jeans. A white shirt. A toothbrush.

And the photograph. He slipped it into his shirt pocket like contraband, feeling the stiff edge of the paper against his chest, right over his heart.

He drove to the World Trade Center terminal. He left the car in a garage that smelled of salt and exhaust fumes.

He walked toward the ferry.

The seagulls wheeled overhead. *Cree-cree.* They cried as if they had read the first draft of this story and found it lacking.

Harold boarded. He stood at the railing.

The ship lurched away from the dock. The engines roared. The city of Boston shrank to a line of Lego bricks on the horizon.

Harold let the wind prickle his neck.

He tried to rehearse a greeting.

"Hello, Patrick." No. Too formal. "It's been a long time." Obvious. "I missed you." Too true.

Nothing arrived intact.

He told himself he had crossed an ocean once for less. He told himself that water was just water, and the past was a country you could visit without applying for a visa.

But the truth sat heavier in his stomach.

He was travelling toward the one person who had never required translation. The one person who spoke the language of silence fluently.

And Harold had no idea what words he would use when they were finally in the same room.

Halfway through the journey, the fog rolled in.

It erased the horizon. It erased the certainty of the destination.

The ferry slowed. The engines dropped to a murmur. *Thrum... thrum...*

The other passengers vanished inside the cabin, pulling their jackets tight against the damp.

Harold stayed outside.

He pressed his hand against his shirt pocket. He could feel the outline of the photograph.

He stared into the whiteout.

Through the fog, he imagined Patrick. He imagined him on the opposite deck, brush in hand, painting the fog itself. Painting the invisible ferry. Painting the invisible thread that connected them, the thread that had stretched and frayed but had never quite broken.

The engines cut out completely. The ship drifted.

Harold closed his eyes.

He listened.

Water slapping against the steel. *Slap. Slap.* Seagulls overhead. His own heart, keeping time like a metronome set too fast. *Tick-tick-tick.*

Somewhere inside the white, a bell rang. Thin and clear. A buoy.

Harold opened his eyes.

He understood then that arrival was not a place. Arrival was a decision.

It was a decision you made with your eyes open. With empty hands. With a mouth ready to pronounce the first syllable of a name you had carried for half your life.

The fog parted.

It happened as suddenly as it had arrived. The curtain lifted.

Provincetown appeared.

It was a cluster of wooden houses, shoulder to shoulder, painted in greys and whites. A long pier reached out into the bay like an offered hand.

The ferry's engine roared back to life, churning the water white.

Harold waited until the gangway crashed down.

He stepped onto the planks. The wood vibrated beneath his feet.

The salt wind lifted his hair: the hair Patrick used to say defied gravity.

Harold checked the photograph one last time, secure against his pulse.

He scanned the crowd on the pier.

He had no plan beyond the next sentence. He had no map beyond the face waiting somewhere inside that crowd.

It was enough.

It had to be.

Chapter XII

When the Heart Returns

The gangway hit the pier with a heavy, industrial metallic clang: the sound of a drawbridge coming down over a moat.

Harold Carrington stood on the deck of the *Provincetown II.* The fog that had swallowed the journey was beginning to burn off, peeling away in ragged, ghostly strips to reveal the town in sharp, high-definition colour.

He saw the long wooden pier reaching out into the harbour like a splinter in the thumb of the water. He saw the cluster of clapboard houses, white and grey, crowded against the shoreline like barnacles clinging to a ship's hull. He saw the Pilgrim Monument rising like a stone needle against a sky that was rapidly turning the colour of a robin's egg: a fragile, brittle blue.

He took a breath. The air smelled of brine, fried clams, and low tide. It smelled of exposure.

He gripped the handle of his small leather weekend bag until his knuckles turned white. Inside his chest, his heartbeat with an erratic rhythm, lurching like a train carriage coupling too fast. *Thump-clack. Thump-clack.*

Walk, he told himself. *Just walk.*

He joined the stream of disembarking passengers. Tourists in bright windbreakers dragging wheeled suitcases that rumbled like distant thunder. Drag queens in sequins shielding their wigs from the wind with manicured hands. Men holding hands. Women holding hands.

Harold moved with them, a tall man in a navy-blue blazer and sensible shoes, looking entirely out of place in this carnival of freedom. He was a piece of brutalist architecture dropped into a watercolour painting.

He reached the end of the pier. The crowd began to disperse into the chaos of Commercial Street, absorbed by the shops and the noise.

And then he saw him.

Patrick was leaning against a wooden piling near the bicycle racks.

He was not looking at the boat. He was looking at the ground, scuffing the toe of a canvas trainer against the gravel, kicking at stones that were not there.

He looked older. That was Harold's first, terrified thought. *We are old. The erosion has begun.*

Patrick's hair, once a dark, chaotic mane that defied physics, was now silvered at the temples and cut shorter. He wore jeans the colour of dried ink and a grey sweater that was fraying slightly at the cuffs. He looked weathered. He looked like something the sea had washed up and decided to keep.

But then Patrick looked up.

The eyes were the same. Dark. Startled. Holding the light as if it were a puzzling question he was waiting to answer. The same downward tension at the corner of his mouth that suggested thoughts arriving faster than words could catch them.

Harold stopped. The crowd flowed around him like water around a rock.

Patrick pushed himself off the piling. He did not smile. He simply stood there, hands in his pockets, staring.

"Harry?"

The nickname slipped out. It was not a question. It was a verification. A password spoken at a border crossing.

Harold nodded. His throat felt useless, stuffed with cotton.

"I found you," Harold managed to say. The words sounded like a confession. Or a plea.

Patrick took a step forward. He stopped. He looked at Harold's blazer. He looked at the sensible shoes. He looked at the face that had aged in a different time zone.

"You're late," Patrick said softly.

Harold blinked.

"The fog... the ferry was delayed."

"No," Patrick said. A small, crooked smile appeared like a ghost on his face, breaking the weather. "I mean... generally."

Harold let out a breath he felt he had been holding since 1991.

"Yes. I suppose I am."

"My place is this way," Patrick said. "East End. It's quiet."

They walked.

They walked side by side down Commercial Street. It was a narrow lane shared by pedestrians, cyclists, and the occasional slow-moving car.

They passed gardens overflowing with blue hydrangeas the size of human heads, bobbing in the breeze like drowned balloons. They passed white picket fences that guarded nothing. They passed galleries where paintings of dunes and light hung in the windows, promising a peace neither of them possessed.

They did not touch. They did not speak. The silence between them was not empty; it was heavy, vibrating with twenty years of unspoken sentences. It was a physical weight, a third person walking between them.

Harold noticed that their walking rhythm—that syncopated *scuff, step, scuff, step* of childhood—was gone. They were out of phase. Patrick walked with a loose, wandering gait, following the drift of the sand. Harold walked with a city stride, efficient and direct, marching toward a deadline that no longer existed.

They had to learn how to walk together again.

Patrick turned down a side lane lined with crushed seashells that crunched like bones underfoot. He stopped at a small, weather-beaten shingle cottage. It sat slightly askew, as if it had settled comfortably into the dunes for a nap.

"It's a rental," Patrick said, unlocking the door. "But the light is good."

They went inside.

The studio—it was just the main room of the cottage—smelled of turpentine, fresh coffee, and the sea.

Easels stood like witnesses in the corners. The floor was covered with a drop cloth that was a map of every colour Patrick had used that summer. Cerulean. Ochre. A violent, shocking pink that looked like a fresh bruise.

Patrick dropped his keys into a bowl. *Clack.*

He turned to face Harold.

The cottage was small. Suddenly, they were close. Too close. The air between them thinned.

"So," Patrick said. He crossed his arms, a defensive gesture, building a wall. "You saw the painting."

"Thomas saw it," Harold corrected. "My son. He has better eyes than I do."

"Thomas." Patrick weighed the name on his tongue. "You have a son."

"And a daughter. Sarah. She is sixteen."

Patrick nodded slowly. He looked at Harold's face, reading the map of the years he had missed. The lines around the eyes. The set of the jaw. The way grief had carved him into something sharper.

"And your wife?" Patrick asked. "Eleanor?"

"We divorced," Harold said. "Six years ago."

Patrick's eyebrows rose.

"I am sorry."

"Don't be," Harold said. He looked at the floor, then back at Patrick. "She told me to find what I was looking for. She knew before I did."

Patrick went to the small kitchenette. He flicked the kettle on. It was a reflex. Something to do with his hands.

"Tea?" Patrick asked.

"Please."

"I don't have Earl Grey. Only builder's tea."

"That is fine."

Harold watched him. He watched the way Patrick moved: efficient, fluid. He watched the way Patrick's shoulder blades shifted beneath the grey sweater, clipped wings still trying to open.

"Why didn't you answer?" Harold asked. "After I called your mother? Years ago."

Patrick froze. He did not turn around.

"I didn't know what to say," Patrick whispered to the kettle. "You said you didn't want to disrupt my momentum. I thought... I thought you wanted me to keep going. Away from you."

"I wanted you to fly," Harold said. "I didn't want to be the gravity holding you down."

Patrick turned around then. His eyes were wet.

"Harry," he said. "You weren't gravity. You were ground control. I was just spinning out there."

Harold reached into the pocket of his blazer.

He felt the paper. Stiff. Familiar. Warmer than his hand.

He pulled it out.

The photograph.

It was faded, the edges soft from handling. Pitshanger Park, 1987. Two boys laughing at a heron, unaware that the sky was about to fall in.

He held it out.

Patrick stared at it. He stopped breathing.

He saw the boys they used to be. And in the corner, he saw the absurd, tiny red bus he had painted with the last drop of cochineal pigment in 2005.

"You kept it," Patrick said. His voice broke.

"I tried to throw it away," Harold admitted. "Three times. Once when I got married. Once when Eleanor left. Once when I saw the painting online."

"But you didn't."

"No. I couldn't."

Harold took a step forward. He offered the photo properly now.

Patrick reached out. His hand was trembling. Paint—dried cobalt blue—stained his thumb.

He took the paper. He ran his thumb over the painted bus.

"It is real," Patrick whispered. "I painted it so many times I started to think I had invented it. That I had invented us."

"You didn't invent us," Harold said.

He stepped closer. He was inside Patrick's personal space now. He could smell the linseed oil. He could smell the soap Patrick used. He could smell the loneliness that had settled into the wool of the sweater.

"I am sorry," Harold said. "I am sorry about the launderette. I am sorry about the silence. I am sorry I was so afraid of the curve that I tried to live in a straight line for twenty years."

Patrick looked up at him. He clutched the photograph to his chest like a shield.

"You are here now," Patrick said.

"I am."

Harold raised his hands. He hesitated for a fraction of a second: the old fear, the old programming kicking in. Structure. Rules. Boundaries. Do not touch the artwork.

Then he broke the rule.

He took Patrick's face in his hands.

He felt the stubble on Patrick's jaw. He felt the heat of the skin. He felt the pulse jumping at Patrick's temple, a frantic Morse code.

"I crossed an ocean," Harold said, his voice low and steady. "I took a plane, a train, and a ferry. But the real distance was shorter than this."

He leaned in.

He pressed his forehead against Patrick's.

Rest against rest. Bone against bone.

Patrick let out a sound: half-sob, half-laugh. He leaned into the touch. The photograph was pressed between their chests, the paper bending but not breaking.

"I missed you," Patrick whispered into the space between them. "God, I missed you."

"I know," Harold said. "I am sorry it took me so long to find the exit."

They stood there for a long time. The kettle began to boil, whistling its hysterical aria, screaming for attention, but neither of them moved to turn it off. They simply stood there, letting the thread pull taut, stitching the years back together, one minute at a time.

Later, the light changed.

The afternoon slipped into the "golden hour"—that specific, melancholic light that painters flock to Provincetown for. The studio turned a deep, dusty rose, as if the air itself were blushing.

They sat on the floor, their backs against the radiator, just as they had in the university launderette.

They didn't kiss. Not yet. The intimacy of simply being was overwhelming enough.

They ate dinner sitting on the floor. Patrick had gone to a shack on the pier and brought back lobster rolls wrapped in foil and a bottle of cold white wine.

They ate with their hands.

"So," Patrick said, wiping mayonnaise from his lip. "You are a partner now."

"I was," Harold said. "I handed in my notice before I left."

Patrick stopped chewing.

"You quit?"

"I asked for a sabbatical. Indefinite." Harold took a sip of wine. "The billable hours started to feel like borrowed time, Pat. I was measuring my life in six-minute increments, and none of them were mine."

"What will you do?"

"I don't know." Harold smiled. It was a real smile. It reached his eyes. "I thought I might learn to draw. I have this watercolour set. Barely used."

Patrick laughed. It was the laugh from the lilac bush. Sharp and bright.

"I know a teacher," Patrick said. "He is expensive, though. He demands payment in wine and attention."

"I can afford him."

After dinner, they walked.

The town had transformed. The day-trippers had returned on the ferry. The streets belonged to the locals and the stayers now.

The air was cool. Harold wore his blazer.

Patrick went to the coat rack near the door. He reached for a scarf.

It was grey cashmere. Old. Soft as dust. The same scarf Harold had looped around his neck in a graveyard in 1998.

Patrick wound it around his neck. He caught Harold looking at it.

"It's good wool," Patrick said simply. "Lasts a lifetime."

They walked to the end of the breakwater. The tide was out. The sand flats stretched for miles, reflecting the moon like a shattered mirror.

Harold shoved his hands into his pockets. He felt the phantom weight of his phone, of his emails, of his obligations. They felt extremely far away.

He looked at Patrick. The grey scarf looked bright against the dark water.

"Thomas is a good boy," Harold said suddenly. "He found the painting. Practically shoved the phone in my face."

"I'll have to thank him," Patrick said.

"He wants to be a filmmaker. He likes... narrative."

Patrick bumped his shoulder against Harold's.

"Get that from you."

"I am an actuary of the soul, Patrick. I don't do narrative."

"You do," Patrick said. "You just write it in invisible ink. But I always read it."

At the street corner where the path turned back toward the cottage, the streetlamp hummed.

Harold stopped.

He turned to Patrick.

The humour faded from Patrick's face. He looked at Harold with that same terrifying openness.

Harold took his hands out of his pockets. He reached out and took Patrick's hand.

He threaded their fingers together.

It wasn't the desperate grip of the fallen tree. It wasn't the fearful clutching of the launderette.

It was a grasp. Firm. Certain.

"I am not going back," Harold said. "Not to the way it was."

Patrick squeezed his hand.

"I know."

Harold looked at the scarf around Patrick's neck. He looked at the red thread that ran invisibly between them.

"Let's walk," Harold said. "The city is wide enough for both of us now. Or the town. Or wherever we are."

Patrick smiled.

"We are here, Harry. We are finally here."

They stepped off the curb together.

They walked into the pool of light beneath the streetlamp, and then out the other side, into the shadows, into the future.

The red thread was no longer a line on a canvas. It was no longer a ghost in a drawer. It was just a feeling, keeping them warm against the Atlantic chill, as they walked home.

Chapter XIII

Threads of a Shared Canvas

Patrick woke to the silence of a London morning, the kind that arrives in a bruised, apologetic pink after a night of heavy rain.

It was May of 2012.

The light slipped through the linen curtains—curtains they had chosen together at John Lewis, arguing for twenty minutes over the difference between 'oatmeal' and 'stone'—and painted the bedsheets the colour of watered-down milk.

Beside him, Harold was breathing.

It was a slow, steady rhythm. In... out. One of Harold's arms was thrown across the duvet, heavy and proprietary, as if claiming a continent.

For a long moment, Patrick did nothing. He just listened.

He heard the distant, oceanic hum of traffic on the North Circular. He heard the soft, metallic *click-tick* of the radiator cooling down. He smelled the faint scent of cedar and expensive shaving soap that now lived in every room Harold entered.

He closed his eyes again. He was unwilling to trade the warm certainty of Harold's skin for the uncertainty of the day's palette.

Finally, the kettle dragged him to his feet. Harold had bought a vintage whistling kettle that sounded like the shriek of a startled train.

Patrick walked to the kitchen. The floorboards were cold. He wore mismatched socks: one navy-blue, one grey.

He made the coffee. Strong for Harold. With milk for himself.

He carried the mugs back to the bedroom like offerings.

Harold stirred. He smiled without opening his eyes, burying his face deeper into the pillow.

"I dreamed you were painting," Harold murmured, his voice thick with sleep. "But the canvas kept changing. Every time you drew a line, the colours rearranged themselves into memories."

Patrick placed the mugs on the windowsill.

"Perhaps the paper is tired of being still," he said. "Perhaps it wants to answer back."

Harold opened one eye.

"Do you always have to be profound before 8:00 a.m.?"

"It is my job. I am an artist."

They drank coffee in bed, sitting up against the headboard, their knees touching beneath the duvet. The quilt formed a small, warm country between them.

Outside, a postman whistled out of tune. A woman pushed a pram over the cracked pavement, the wheels rattling.

Patrick looked out the window. His brush hand twitched against the ceramic mug. He was already translating the scene—the bruised light, the wet brick—into cadmium orange and Payne's Grey.

Bzzzz.

Harold's phone vibrated on the bedside table.

Harold groaned. He picked it up.

"Email from Chambers," he said. "Subject line: Mediation: Cheese Dispute."

Patrick laughed. He nearly spilled his coffee.

"Pardon?"

Harold rolled his eyes. His thumb hovered over the delete button before he thought better of it.

"Artisan cheddar," Harold muttered. "Two dairies in Somerset. They are arguing over mould rights. One of them owns the specific bacterial culture used in the cave."

Patrick laughed again. The sound surprised him. It was loose, unthinking. As if someone else had lent him their throat for the morning.

"You spent twenty years working on multinational mergers," Patrick said. "You structured the debt for skyscrapers. And now you are mediating over mould?"

"Mould has opinions, Patrick. It is a living organism. It is highly litigious."

Harold finished his coffee. He kissed the top of Patrick's head. He stood up, stretching until his vertebrae clicked. *Crack.*

"I have to be at the Temple by ten," Harold said. "Don't paint anything too beautiful before I get back. I will miss the reveal."

Patrick watched him dress. He watched Harold tie his tie: a Windsor knot, perfect every time. He watched him put on his cufflinks.

"Go," Patrick said. "Defend the cheese."

After Harold left, the studio settled into its familiar silence.

They had rented a flat in Maida Vale with high ceilings and a spare room that faced north. This was the studio.

Patrick turned to the easel. A half-finished landscape called to him.

His recent work had changed. The critics in New York had called it "restrained melancholy." But the new work...

It had taken on a vitality he hadn't planned. Sunnier yellows. Hopeful greens. A surprising amount of lavender: an unconscious homage to his mother's garden in Ealing, and perhaps to the tender blooming of his own heart.

He worked for four hours.

The rhythmic scrape of the brush against the canvas was a meditation. *Scrape... tap... swirl.*

He thought of Harold. He imagined him sitting in a wood-panelled room, navigating legal clauses about bacteria. He thought of their vastly different languages—Law and Art—and yet, how perfectly they converged at the end of each day. Harold provided the frame; Patrick provided the picture.

At 2:00 p.m., the telephone rang.

It was Elena, calling from New York.

"Darling," her voice crackled on the line, sharp as a dry martini glass. "I have the proofs for the catalogue. And the critics are raving about the previews."

"Are they?" Patrick wiped a brush on a rag.

"They are calling the new work 'A Dawn for Evans.' Which is a bit melodramatic, even for me, but it sells. We must schedule another exhibition. October? London this time?"

Patrick smiled. A genuine warmth spread through him.

"London sounds good," he said. "I am here. I am staying."

"Good. You sound... light, Patrick. You sound lighter."

"I am," Patrick said.

After hanging up, he felt a surge of satisfaction. For so long, his art had been a solitary dialogue with his own confusion. A way of bleeding onto the page.

Now, it felt like an offering. He felt emboldened by a love that had found its way back to him against all odds.

Evening arrived with the soft jingle of Harold's key in the lock.

It was the best sound in the world.

They cooked together.

Harold chopped onions with forensic precision. Patrick tossed pasta into boiling water with careless abandon.

They made a sauce with too much garlic and too much chilli. They ate on the sofa, their legs tangled together, balancing bowls on their knees.

They discussed everything and nothing.

"The neighbour's cat was on the balcony again," Patrick said. "It thinks it lives here."

"It has squatter's rights by now," Harold said. "Adverse possession."

"And the cheese?"

"Resolved. They agreed to share the bacteria. It was a joint custody battle."

Later, the room grew dark. Harold switched on the lamp. He put on his reading glasses and opened a folder of briefs.

Patrick picked up his sketchbook.

He sketched Harold.

He drew the line of the jaw. He drew the way the lamplight settled on the curve of Harold's ear. He drew the small, vertical frown line that appeared between Harold's eyebrows whenever the law grew ambiguous.

Patrick worked quickly. Economical lines. He didn't need to look hard; his hand knew the topography of Harold's face better than it knew the streets of London.

Before going to sleep, they stood in the bathroom.

Harold placed his palm against Patrick's cheek. His thumb brushed the smudge of Phthalo Green that always lingered on Patrick's cheekbone, no matter how thoroughly he washed.

"Still here," Harold said. His voice was low, filled with wonder.

Patrick covered Harold's hand with his own.

"Still here," Patrick replied.

He turned off the light.

The weeks unfolded in small symphonies.

They established rituals without discussion.

Harold made the coffee strong enough to stand a spoon in. Patrick added milk the colour of weathered stone.

Sunday meant croissants from the Polish bakery down the road. They ate them in bed, dropping crumbs everywhere, reading the Sunday papers.

Wednesday meant late-night jazz on Radio 3.

The first of every month meant stripping the bedding and washing the sheets. They danced barefoot to Nina Simone while the linen billowed on the washing line outside like flags of surrender.

Harold's practice became more austere.

He had left the massive law firm. He had joined a smaller set of Chambers. He took on fewer cases. He chose the ones that let him sleep at night.

He discovered he could draft a contract in the morning and still be home for dinner. He discovered that justice sometimes looked like arriving on time with a bottle of wine and a joke.

His former partners raised their eyebrows when they met him for lunch.

"You look... relaxed, Carrington. Business going poorly?"

Harold would simply raise one shoulder.

"Business is life, John. And life is good."

The corner office felt smaller now. The view of the Thames from their kitchen window felt wide enough to sail an armada through.

Patrick's work shifted into a new key.

The critics called it "The Light Suite."

The colours were deeper than light, however. They were like the memory of light. The moment just before the sunset decides to stay.

He painted Harold reading briefs. He painted the neighbour's cat asleep on Harold's leather briefcase.

He painted the ferry.

He painted the *Provincetown II* cutting through the fog. But this time, the red thread was visible. It wasn't hidden in the underpainting. It was deliberate. It was part of the composition. It connected the boat to the shore.

Elena priced them higher than anything he had ever sold before.

They sold anyway.

The buyers spoke of "hope." They spoke of "quiet jubilation."

Patrick listened to them at the opening. He nodded. He drank the warm wine. Then he went home to wash his brushes, unsure if the joy was on the canvas or simply in the room where it dried.

One evening in late May, they walked along the Thames Embankment.

The sky had been rinsed clean after a storm. The air smelled of ozone and wet pavement. Barges slipped down the river like slow prayers.

Harold was talking about a pro-bono case he had taken on.

"It is ridiculous," Harold said. "The landlord wants to evict a family. Single mother. Two children. Their only crime is that they own a dog. A mongrel. The tenancy agreement says, 'No Pets,' but the dog is practically a therapy animal for the youngest boy."

Patrick listened. He watched the light hit the water.

"Paint them," Patrick said.

Harold laughed. "I do not paint, Pat. You know that."

"You could. You see edges that I miss. The law is just another way of drawing a line, isn't it? You trace a boundary. You create a space."

"I suppose."

They stopped at a chip stall near the Tate. They bought a portion of chips wrapped in paper. They ate leaning against the balustrade, the vinegar sharp in the air.

Seagulls wheeled overhead, crying like rusted hinges.

Harold reached out. He licked the salt from his own fingers. Then, without thinking, he reached out and licked a grain of salt from Patrick's thumb, where a chip had left a smear of grease.

It was a small gesture. Public. Irrelevant to the passing tourists.

But to Patrick, it was a cathedral. It was the kind of casual intimacy that took thirty years to build.

Later, at home, Harold was quiet.

He went to the hall cupboard. He pulled out the battered old tin of Winsor & Newton watercolours: the one he had given Patrick in 1998; the one Patrick had returned to him in 2005.

He set it on the kitchen table.

"All right," Harold said. "Teach me."

They sat at the table. Patrick filled a jar with water.

"We are painting the dog," Patrick said. "The one from the case."

Harold wet the brush. His hand, usually so steady with a pen, wavered.

"I don't know the shape," Harold said.

"You don't need the shape. You need the feeling. Is it sad? Is it loyal?"

"It is... worried," Harold said. "It knows it is a problem."

Harold painted. He used brown. He used ochre.

The colours ran. The lines were shaky. The dog emerged earnest and crooked. It had one ear up and one ear down. It had eyes that had seen eviction notices before.

Harold leaned back. He looked at it critically.

"It is a disaster," Harold said.

"It is perfect," Patrick said.

Patrick took a fridge magnet, one shaped like a Lisbon tram. He pinned the wet painting to the refrigerator door.

They stood back, their arms around each other's waists.

"It adds character to the kitchen," Patrick said.

"It looks like a potato with legs," Harold said. But he was smiling.

They stood there, admiring the law that their collaboration had just rewritten. The dog would stay. The family would stay. And the painting would stay on the fridge.

Before bed, Harold stood at the bathroom sink.

He was rinsing the old brush.

The water turned pink. Then lavender. Then clear.

Patrick watched him from the doorway. His toothbrush was idle in his hand. His heart was full of the ordinary miracle of shared plumbing.

Harold turned off the tap. The towel still bore a faint, permanent stain of Ultramarine Blue from Patrick's face wash.

Harold looked at Patrick in the mirror.

"I like this version of us," Harold said.

Patrick stepped into the room. He pressed a kiss to the back of Harold's neck.

"Me too," Patrick whispered. "It is my favourite period. The Blue Period. The

Red Period. And now... The Us Period."

Harold turned around. He embraced Patrick.

Outside, the London rain began again, drumming against the glass, sealing them in.

Chapter XIV

Echoes in the Hum of the City

Harold's day began with the reluctant, metallic sigh of the bedroom radiator.

It was followed by the low, oceanic murmur of London waking up outside the sash window. The whine of an electric milk float. The harsh cry of seagulls drifting inland from the Thames, sounding like rusted hinges swinging in the wind. The distant, subterranean rumble of the Bakerloo line rushing beneath the street like a long, satisfied sigh in the throat of the earth.

Harold lay still for a moment, cataloguing the sounds. It was a habit he could not break. Identify. Categorize. File away.

Beside him, Patrick was a warm, motionless shape beneath the duvet. Patrick slept like the dead: deep, dreamless, and sprawled out. He had claimed the last inch of warmth in the bed, curling himself into a shape that defied spinal geometry, a question mark sketched in linen.

Harold slipped out of bed. The floorboards were cold, snapping against his bare feet.

He dressed in the gloom of the hallway so as not to wake Patrick. He put on a crisp white shirt. He selected a tie.

Patrick had chosen this one. He had held it up in the shop on Jermyn Street and said, "It is the colour of wet slate, Harry. Or a dove's wing in the rain. It's perfect."

Harold knotted the wet-slate tie. He checked his reflection in the hallway mirror. He looked like a partner at an exclusive law firm. But he knew that beneath his shirt cuff, on his left wrist, was a small smudge of Phthalo Blue paint that hadn't quite washed off from last night's impromptu lesson. A secret tattoo.

He watched the city assemble itself beyond the window.

Maida Vale was waking up. Delivery vans were double-parked on the Crescent, their hazard lights blinking in a syncopated rhythm. A bakery van dispensed trays of croissants to the corner café, the yeasty aroma rising like a prayer. A woman in neon pink Lycra power-walked with a terrier that looked permanently scandalized by the pace.

Harold returned to the bedroom. He leaned over the bed.

He kissed Patrick's temple. It was warm and smelled of sleep and cedar.

"I am leaving," Harold whispered.

Patrick grunted. He shifted, burying his face deeper into the pillow.

"Mmph. Defend the cheese."

Harold smiled.

"I will."

He stepped out into the morning chill.

The walk to the Warwick Avenue tube station was seven minutes. Harold had timed it twice when they first moved in. Then, he had stopped timing it. He was trying, consciously, not to be the kind of man who timed things. He was trying to be the kind of man who noticed the way the light hit the wet pavement, turning the tarmac into a mirror.

He stopped at the Polish bakery on the corner.

The air inside was thick with yeast and icing sugar.

"Good morning, Mr. Carrington," the girl behind the counter said.

"Good morning, Kasia. Just black coffee. And one of the cardamom buns. A warm one."

He bought the coffee. It was strong enough to stand a spoon in. He bought the bun, wrapping the paper bag around it to keep his hands warm. He wouldn't eat it yet. He would eat it at his desk, a small act of rebellion against the sterility of the office.

He descended into the Underground.

The station smelled of ozone and damp dust.

The train was packed but polite. The commuters stood shoulder to shoulder, their newspapers rustling like dry leaves. *Rustle. Snap. Turn.*

Harold stood near the doors; his leather briefcase wedged between his shoes.

He opened his file. Case 409: The Cheddar Gorge Dispute.

It was absurd. Two artisan cheesemakers in Somerset were arguing over the patent rights to a specific strain of blue mould. *Penicillium roqueforti.*

Harold read the testimonies. They were vitriolic. They were passionate.

"The respondent's claim that the veining is natural is a fabrication. That specific marbling pattern is the result of my grandfather's piercing technique..."

Harold underlined a phrase: "Naturally occurring veins of blue."

He smiled. He looked at the hair loss treatment advertisement above the window.

He wondered how he had arrived at a life where fungi required litigation.

Twenty years ago, he had been structuring debt for skyscrapers in Dubai. He had been moving millions of pounds across borders with a keystroke. Now, he was arguing over spores.

And he was happier.

Patrick would love this. Patrick would paint the mould. He would paint it a triumphant, regal Cerulean Blue and hang it above the sofa, titling it *The Litigious Spore.*

At Liverpool Street, he surfaced.

The sunlight was weak, filtering through the high clouds like watered-down milk.

He joined the river of coats flowing toward the financial district. Black coats. Navy-blue coats. Grey coats. A sea of wool and cashmere moving toward the glass towers that reflected one another in endless, narcissistic approval.

Harold entered his building. He nodded to the security guard.

In the lift up to the thirty-second floor, he stood beside two men from the corporate department.

"Good morning, Harold," one said. "Did you see the FTSE?"

"Flat," Harold said.

They nodded. They knew him as the quiet partner. The one who drafted contracts as taut as drumheads. The one who never came to Friday drinks. The one whose private life remained politely unexamined, a blank space in the office gossip.

They did not know that last night, Harold had sat at a kitchen table mixing paint on a chipped plate. They did not know that he had helped Patrick render a dog's ear the exact lavender of the sunset, his own hand trembling slightly until Patrick covered it with his own.

He preferred the imbalance. He liked having a secret room they could not enter.

His office overlooked the Thames.

The tide was out. The mud was exposed, shining like oil. The seagulls were picking over the secrets the river had discarded.

Harold set down his coffee. He hung his overcoat on the back of the door.

He unwound the grey cashmere scarf from his neck—the one Patrick had worn on the pier, the one they now shared without asking—and draped it over his blazer. It smelled faintly of Patrick's cologne.

He unwrapped the cardamom bun. The smell of spices filled the sterile, air-conditioned room.

He opened the file.

The words organized themselves into clauses. The clauses into paragraphs.

The paragraphs into certainty.

"Therefore, the parties agree to a shared licence with respect to the bacterial culture..."

He worked with the steady rhythm of someone who has learned that justice is often the art of making unimportant things fit together so people can sleep at night. He built the contract like a wall. Brick by brick.

At half past ten, his phone alarm vibrated.

He picked up the landline. He dialled the studio number.

It rang three times.

"Studio," Patrick's voice answered. He sounded rough, distracted.

"Are you still alive?" Harold asked.

"Barely. I am wrestling with a skyline. It keeps wanting to tilt."

"Let it tilt," Harold said. "Call it perspective."

"How is the world of high finance?"

"Currently fungal. The mould people are suing each other over the spore count."

Patrick laughed. The sound came through the line, warm as the cardamom bun.

"Paint them a settlement, Harry. Ultramarine with a touch of forgiveness."

"I am drafting it now. I am proposing a dual-branding strategy. Brother Cheeses."

"You are a genius."

"I am a lawyer. It is similar, but with more paperwork."

They spoke for three minutes. Long enough for Harold to hear a brush being swished in a jar of water. *Swish-swish-tink.* Long enough for the office to feel less like a glass cage and more like a skin he could shed.

"See you later," Patrick said.

"See you."

When Harold hung up, his secretary, Maria, was standing in the doorway holding a file. She was smiling.

"You look cheerful, Mr. Carrington," she said.

Harold touched his tie.

"Do I?"

"Yes. It suits you."

Lunch was a sandwich eaten on the stone steps by the river.

The wind whipped Harold's tie like a flag whose country no longer existed. He watched the tourists photographing each other with Tower Bridge in the background. Their outlines were soft in the milky light.

A young boy, about five years old, dropped his ice cream cone. *Splat.*

The boy's face crumbled. The tragedy was absolute.

Harold watched the mother. She did not scold him. She knelt. She pulled a tissue from her bag. She wiped away the tears. Then, she broke her own cone in half and offered the boy the larger piece.

Harold felt the scene settle inside him like evidence.

Exhibit A.

People managed to repair one another every day without contracts. They balanced the books with kindness, not litigation.

He finished his sandwich. He crumpled the foil wrapper into a ball. He felt light.

The afternoon brought the mediation.

The cheesemakers arrived at 2:00 p.m.

They were two stubborn men in tweed jackets, each accompanied by a solicitor in a cheap suit. They sat on opposite sides of the mahogany conference table.

They had brought samples. Wheels of cheddar wrapped in wax paper sat on the polished wood, looking out of place among the MacBooks.

"He stole the blue," Mr. Henderson said, pointing a calloused finger. "That culture has been in my family's cave since 1920."

"It is airborne!" Mr. Davies shouted. "The spores travel! I can't tell the wind where to blow!"

Harold raised a hand.

"Gentlemen," he said. His voice was low, calm. The architect's voice. "Let us look at the structure of the problem."

He listened. He let them shout for twenty minutes. He let the anger drain from the room.

Then, he translated their disappointment into a language they could both sign.

"Shared heritage." "Regional protection." "Joint venture."

He drew a diagram on his legal pad. He showed them how two circles could overlap to create a stronger shape.

By 4:00 p.m., they were tired. They were hungry.

They shook hands.

"I suppose," Mr. Henderson grumbled, "we could do a gift box. The Valley Collection."

"I suppose," Mr. Davies agreed.

On their way out, Mrs. Henderson, a quiet woman who had sat in the corner taking notes, pressed a small wheel of the disputed cheese into Harold's palm.

"For your wife," she said kindly. "She will like this one. It is very sharp."

Harold looked at the cheese. He looked at the woman.

He did not correct her. He did not say, "I have no wife. I have a partner named Patrick who paints skylines that tilt."

He didn't say it because he didn't need to. He didn't need her validation to make Patrick real. Their truth no longer required a witness to exist.

"Thank you," Harold said. "I am sure it will be appreciated."

He carried the cheese home like a diplomatic pouch. The wheel was wrapped in brown paper, cool and heavy against his palm inside his briefcase.

The Underground was packed again. Rush hour.

He stood shoulder to shoulder with strangers who smelled of wet wool, exhaustion, and resignation.

Usually, Harold would read. But tonight, he found himself studying faces.

He was looking at them the way Patrick studied a still life.

He looked at the woman opposite him. Her mascara had run into dark circles like bruised commas beneath her eyes. *Solid Blue*, he thought. *Darker than guilt.*

He looked at the boy asleep against his backpack. The line of his jaw was sharp, vulnerable.

He looked at the old man humming a melody under his breath. Harold almost recognized it. *Greensleeves?*

Each of them carried a private canvas. Harold felt the weight of the brushes they would never pick up. He felt a sudden, fierce gratitude that he had been given a second chance to pick up his own.

At Warwick Avenue, he surfaced into the evening.

The streetlamps were buzzing as they flickered on. Amber. Pink.

He walked past the canal. The water was black, reflecting the weeping willows.

The bakery was closing. Its lights dimming like a stage after the final curtain.

Harold bought two croissants for tomorrow morning. He accepted Kasia's last change.

He walked the final streets toward the flat. The plane trees dropped leaves the colour of burnt caramel onto the pavement. *Scuff, step. Scuff, step.*

He looked up.

The third-floor window glowed a buttery yellow.

He could see the silhouette.

Patrick was standing in front of the easel. His arm moved in a steady, rhythmic arc. He was building a world from scratch, stroke by stroke.

Harold stopped on the pavement. He just watched for a moment. He watched the man he loved creating something out of nothing.

Inside, the flat smelled of turpentine and roasted garlic.

Patrick did not look up when Harold walked in. He was deep in the zone.

"I mixed the colour of the mould," Patrick told the canvas. "I am calling it Litigation Grey. It dries darker."

Harold laughed. He took off his overcoat. He hung the grey scarf on the hook.

"I brought evidence," Harold said.

He unwrapped the cheese. He placed it on the wooden board in the kitchen.

"We will eat it before it hardens," Harold said. "That is the settlement."

Patrick put down his brush. He took a deep breath and walked into the kitchen. He kissed Harold. A smear of blue paint transferred to Harold's cheek.

"You won," Patrick said.

"We compromised. It is better."

They ate at the small table. Their knees bumped. *Knock. Knock.*

The conversation was loose as a brushstroke.

Patrick talked about the new canvas: London at dawn seen from the window of a night bus. "It's all bruised violet and sodium flare," he said. "It is ugly and it is beautiful."

Harold talked about the woman on the train with the mascara commas.

"You are seeing it," Patrick said, cutting a slice of the sharp cheese. "You are seeing the edges."

"I try."

They laughed, their mouths full. It was the way people laugh when they realize the world has carried on happening while they were busy looking the other way, and they haven't missed the important parts after all.

Later, the plates were stacked.

"We are out of milk," Patrick announced, looking inside the fridge.

"Corner shop?"

"Corner shop."

They put their coats back on. Harold wound the grey scarf around Patrick's neck this time.

They stepped out into the crisp air. The street was quiet. The terrier was gone. The neon-Lycra woman was gone.

A man in a delivery jacket was smoking beneath the awning of the newsagent's.

They bought milk. A bar of dark chocolate. A newspaper that neither of them would read, but which felt good to carry tucked under an arm.

On the way back, they walked close.

Patrick slipped his hand inside the pocket of Harold's overcoat.

Harold felt Patrick's fingers. They were warm. They found the space between Harold's keys and his loose change. They curled around the small, cold handle of the cheese knife Harold had absentmindedly pocketed after clearing the table.

They walked like that. Without speaking.

Their footsteps echoed against the brick of the terraced houses. *Click-clack. Click-clack.*

The city hummed its indifferent lullaby all around them. It did not care about them. And that was fine. They were their own city now.

Back at the flat, they left the milk in the hallway.

They took off their shoes.

They stood at the living room window, looking out at the same street they had walked a hundred times.

Somewhere, a siren doppler away. *Nee-naw.*

Somewhere, a dog barked once.

Harold felt the day settle inside him. It felt like coins dropping into a glass jar. *Clink.* Small denominations. Mundane moments. But eventually, they would add up to something worth having. A fortune.

He watched Patrick's reflection in the glass.

"Same again tomorrow?" Patrick asked.

Harold looked at the reflection. Two men. Older. Tired. Home.

"Same again," Harold replied.

And he meant it.

Same city. Same footsteps. The same ordinary miracle of walking home together through the hum of a place that had finally learned their names and was prepared, tonight, to let them keep them.

Chapter XV

The Garden of Time

Saturday arrived soft and edged with salt, the sky over London rinsed clean by a night storm that had dragged its wet sleeves across the rooftops and vanished before dawn.

In the bedroom of the Maida Vale flat, the morning light was not the hard, questioning glare of the office blocks Harold was used to. It was bruised pink and apologetic. It slipped through the linen curtains—oatmeal, heavy weave—and painted the bedsheets the colour of watered-down milk.

Patrick woke first. He lay still for a long time, listening to the specific acoustic signature of the room. He heard the distant, oceanic hum of traffic on the Westway, a sound that always reminded him of waves breaking on a concrete shore. He heard the soft *click-tick* of the radiator cooling down after its morning cycle.

Beside him, Harold was breathing.

It was a slow, steady rhythm. In... out. One of Harold's arms was thrown across the duvet, heavy and proprietary, the hand relaxed, the fingers slightly curled. It was the posture of a man who had finally stopped sleeping like a soldier on high alert.

Patrick slipped out of bed. His bare feet found the stripped pine floorboards, which were cold enough to make him shiver. He walked to the window and looked out.

The street below shone. Raindrops from the storm still clung to the windowpane, sliding down like tiny glass sprinters in a race only they understood.

Behind him, the bed creaked.

Patrick turned around. Harold was stirring. He buried his face deeper into the pillow, groaning softly.

"It is Saturday," Patrick whispered, even though he knew Harold couldn't hear him. "The garden is waiting."

He went to the kitchen.

The cat—a skinny, vocal tabby they had adopted from the shelter three weeks ago—wound around his ankles in demanding figure eights. They hadn't settled on a name yet. Patrick called him Giotto because of the perfect circle he made when he slept; Harold called him Churchill because he was grumpy and demanded meals at inconvenient hours.

Patrick filled the kettle. It was the vintage whistling model Harold had insisted on buying because it was "mechanically sound." It clicked on.

Patrick measured the coffee. He made it the way Harold liked it: dark roast, piled high in the cafetière, water just off the boil. A ritual of precision.

When he carried the mugs back to the bedroom, the room smelled of cedar (Harold's cologne), oil paint (Patrick's skin), and hot, fresh coffee.

Harold rolled over. His hair stood up at the crown, defying the laws of gravity and professional grooming. He looked like a boy.

"Morning," Harold croaked.

"Morning." Patrick placed the mugs on the windowsill. "Drink this. You look like you've been in a fight with the duvet."

Harold sat up, rubbing his eyes.

"I dreamed you were painting," he said, his voice thick with sleep. "But the canvas kept changing. Every time you drew a line, the colours rearranged themselves into memories. I tried to catch them, but my hands were covered in clay."

Patrick sat on the edge of the bed.

"Perhaps the paper is tired of being still," he said softly. "Perhaps it wants to answer back today."

They drank the coffee in bed, their knees touching beneath the duvet. The quilt formed a small, warm country between them, a sovereign state where the only laws were heat and proximity.

Harold's phone vibrated on the bedside table. *Bzzzz.*

He looked at it. He rolled his eyes.

"Email from Chambers," he muttered. "Subject line: Mediation: Cheese Dispute - Update."

Patrick laughed, nearly spilling his coffee.

"They are still at it. I thought you settled the mould custody battle."

"Now they are arguing over marketing rights," Harold said, his thumb hovering over the delete button. "Artisan cheddar is a cutthroat business. They want to know if the font on the label constitutes a breach of contract."

"Delete it," Patrick said. "The mould can wait. Mrs. Gable cannot."

Harold pressed delete. He put the phone face down.

"You are right," Harold said. "Mrs. Gable is a force of nature. She is more terrifying than any High Court judge I have ever faced."

They left the flat at half past ten.

They were dressed for work. Patrick in his paint-splattered jeans and an old jumper. Harold in a pair of chinos that were too new to look casual and a shirt with the sleeves rolled up to the elbows.

They carried offerings. A loaf of sourdough, still warm and dusted with flour, from the Polish bakery on the corner. A jar of dark, expensive honey Harold had bought at a farmers' market in Marylebone, where the vendors still addressed him as "Counsel" even when he was buying vegetables.

They walked to the station. The wind was brisk, stripping the last of the blossom from the cherry trees.

The train journey to Ealing felt like time travel.

As the carriage rattled westward, the city began to revert. The glass towers of the city gave way to the terraced rows of Paddington, which gave way to the leafy, sprawling suburbs.

Harold sat beside Patrick. He held his holdall on his knees. He was looking out the window, but Patrick knew he wasn't seeing the passing houses. He was seeing the past.

"Are you all, right?" Patrick asked quietly.

Harold nodded. He shifted his leg, so his knee pressed against Patrick's. The small pressure was a private language, a Morse code of reassurance.

"I am fine," Harold said. "It is just... strange. Going back there. Without the armour."

"You don't need armour," Patrick said. "It is just a garden."

"It is never just a garden, Pat. It is archaeology."

Ealing Broadway station smelled exactly as it always had ozone, burnt sugar from the waffle stand, and diesel.

They walked the familiar route toward St. Albans Avenue. The streets were busy with Saturday shoppers. Schoolchildren in headphones drifted like ghosts. Mothers pushed prams with the determination of tank commanders.

When they turned onto the avenue, the air changed. It grew quieter. The trees met overhead, forming a tunnel of green that filtered the light.

Number 40—Patrick's old house—was silent. The new owners were in France for the summer, the curtains drawn against the light.

But Number 42 was alive.

Mrs. Gable was waiting for them.

She opened the door before they even reached the bell. It was as if she had been standing there for hours, listening for footsteps that sounded like a reunion.

She was smaller than Patrick remembered. Age had compressed her spine, but her eyes were bright, fierce beads of jet. She wore a cardigan the colour of wet sand, the sleeves rolled up to reveal forearms mapped with veins and scratched by thorns.

"I have been dividing the lavender," she said by way of greeting.

She stepped out onto the porch. She pulled Patrick down for a kiss on the cheek. She smelled of beeswax, lavender soap, and damp earth.

Then, she turned to Harold.

Harold hesitated. He stood up straight, like a schoolboy called to the headmaster's office.

Mrs. Gable did not hesitate. She reached up, grabbed his shoulders, and pulled him down. She kissed his cheek loudly.

"You are too thin," she declared, stepping back to inspect him. "And you have grey in your hair."

"It is the law, Mrs. Gable," Harold said, smiling. "It ages you."

"Nonsense. It is worry. Come in, come in. The garden is having a moment, and I cannot manage the compost heap alone."

They followed her down the short, narrow hallway.

The walls were still lined with photographs. Patrick stopped.

There he was at seven years old, missing a front tooth, holding a cricket bat he couldn't lift. There was his father, holding a spade, looking young and surprised.

And there, in a frame Patrick had not noticed before, was Harold.

A younger Harold. Twelve years old. Caught mid-laugh, head thrown back, sitting on the garden wall.

Harold stopped. He touched the glass of the frame.

"I didn't know she had this," Harold whispered.

"She kept everything," Mrs. Gable called from the kitchen. "Your mother threw things away, Harold. But Olivia... she kept them. Said memories needed shelf space."

The back garden was, indeed, having a moment.

It was an explosion of late-spring growth. The rain had acted like a steroid. The lilacs crowded the back fence in heavy, voluptuous clouds of purple. The hydrangeas bowed their heads, heavy as brides, under the weight of the water.

Mrs. Gable moved among them like a general inspecting the troops. She carried a pair of secateurs that looked lethal. *Snip. Snip.*

"This one survived the frost," she explained, pointing to a stubborn rosebush. "This one did not. Deadheading is a mercy, you know. You must cut away the dead wood to let the new blooms breathe."

She handed Harold a pair of heavy, leather gardening gloves. They were old, stained green.

"The compost bin," she ordered, pointing to the corner. "It is impacted. It needs turning. You have the height for it."

Patrick was given a trowel and a kneeling pad.

"The roses," Mrs. Gable said. "Loosen the soil. Do not damage the roots."

They worked.

For an hour, there was only the sound of labour. The heavy thud of Harold turning the wet, rich compost with a pitchfork. The scrape of Patrick's trowel against the clay. The *snip-snap* of Mrs. Gable's secateurs.

It was mindless work. It was physical. It demanded sweat.

Harold took off his shirt, working in his white undershirt. Patrick watched the muscles of his back move as he lifted the heavy fork. He watched the way the sweat darkened the cotton.

It felt like an exorcism. They were digging up the past, turning it over, letting the air get to it.

"Tea," Mrs. Gable announced at midday. "It is required."

They sat at the wrought-iron table beneath the apple tree. The tree was older now, its bark scarred and gnarled, but it still offered a pool of cool shade.

Mrs. Gable poured from a teapot wearing a knitted cozy. Milk first, the way Patrick's father had always insisted.

Steam rose from the cups, carrying the scent of bergamot and old rituals.

"I have been thinking," Mrs. Gable said. She cradled her cup with both hands, her knuckles swollen. "About time."

She looked at Harold.

"How it used to feel like a corridor you walked down. Straight lines. Doors closing behind you."

She looked at the garden.

"Now, at my age, it is a garden. You turn a corner and you find something you forgot you planted twenty years ago. And there it is. Blooming."

She fixed Harold with a look that pinned him to the chair.

"You were here all along, weren't you?" she said softly. "Just waiting for the weather to change."

Harold's throat closed. He looked down at his tea.

"I was afraid the frost had killed it all, Mrs. Gable," he admitted. "I was afraid I had been away too long."

"Gardens are forgiving," Mrs. Gable said. "They understand late arrivals. And the roots go deep, Harold. Deeper than you think."

They ate the lemon drizzle cake she had baked. It melted on the tongue, the sugar icing sharp enough to make the eyes water. Bees investigated the crumbs, moving heavily from plate to petal.

Patrick watched Mrs. Gable watch Harold. He saw the small, satisfied nod she gave when Harold refilled her cup without being asked.

He felt the day settle inside him. It felt like coins dropping into a jar: small copper denominations of peace that would eventually add up to a fortune.

Later, as the sun began to lower, Mrs. Gable led them to the far corner of the garden.

The lavender here had grown woody. It was old growth, gnarled and thick.

"Dig here," she instructed Patrick.

Patrick looked at the patch of earth near the fence.

"Why?"

"Just dig."

Patrick knelt. He scraped the trowel against the brick-hard clay. *Scrape. Scrape.*

Six inches down, the blade hit metal. *Clang.*

He stopped. He used his hands to brush away the dirt.

He unearthed a biscuit tin. It was an old *Roses* chocolates tin, the metal rusted and flaking, the roses faded to brown ghosts.

"I found this when I was weeding last autumn," Mrs. Gable said. "I buried it again. I thought... I thought you boys should be the ones to bring it into the light."

Patrick pried the lid off. The metal shrieked in protest.

Inside lay two objects.

A marble the colour of storm light, chipped on one side.

And a folded piece of sketching paper. It was damp at the edges, foxed with rust, but intact.

Patrick wiped his hands on his jeans. He unfolded the paper carefully.

It was a drawing.

It was rendered in soft graphite, smudged by time.

Two boys. Fourteen years old. Heads together over a comic book. Shoulders touching. The intimacy of the pose was unmistakable.

Patrick recognized the hand. It wasn't his.

"Mum drew this," Patrick whispered.

He turned it over. On the back, in his mother's looping script:

The Architect and the Artist. Summer, 1987. For when they forget.

Harold looked at the drawing. He reached out and touched the edge of the paper with a trembling finger.

"She saw us," Harold said. His voice broke. "She saw us before we saw ourselves."

"She always saw you, Harold," Mrs. Gable said. "She used to say, 'Those two are like two trees growing from the same root system. You cannot prune one without hurting the other.'"

Harold looked at Patrick. Then at Mrs. Gable. Then at the lavender that needed pruning.

He took a deep breath. He picked up the secateurs.

"Show me what to cut, Mrs. Gable," Harold said, his voice steady now. "I will stay until it is done."

They worked until the evening.

The pile of woody stems grew like evidence of a crime solved.

Patrick carried the clippings to the compost. The scent of broken lavender released memories with every snap.

Crack. Harold's laugh in the treehouse. *Crack.* The smell of November sparklers. *Crack.* The exact, grounding pressure of a palm against his shoulder in a launderette when words had failed.

When the final bush was shaped, Mrs. Gable stepped back. She brushed the dirt from her palms.

"It is done," she pronounced. "The garden is ready for next year."

They left at dusk.

They carried a paper bag of lavender clippings for the flat. Patrick carried the rusted biscuit tin.

At the door, Mrs. Gable pulled them both into a hug that smelled of earth, bergamot, and completion.

"Come back when the blooms open," she said. "They will want to see you together."

On the train home, they sat in the same seats.

The city reversed itself outside the window. The gardens gave way to terraces. Terraces to towers. Towers to the wide, slow curve of the Thames, now reflecting the streetlights like a dark mirror.

Harold held the biscuit tin on his knees. His thumb rubbed the rusted roses.

Neither spoke until the train glided into the tunnel. The darkness enveloped them like an undercoat of primer.

"I thought crossing the ocean was the hard part," Harold said quietly into the dark.

"What was the hard part?" Patrick asked.

"Walking through a door in Ealing," Harold said. "And finding out I hadn't ruined it. That the garden waited."

Patrick rested his head on Harold's shoulder. The bag of lavender between them gave off its sharp, clean ghost.

"We are here now," Patrick replied. "The garden has forgiven us."

They walked back to the flat through streets already lit for the night.

The clippings rustled in their paper bag like small applause. *Shhh-shhh.*

Inside, they didn't turn on the main lights.

They arranged the lavender in mismatched jars: an old jam jar, a cracked pint glass, a vase Patrick had thrown in New York. They placed them on the windowsill where the city light could find them.

Later, when the flat was dark and the hum of the city had dropped to a lullaby, Patrick woke up.

He felt Harold's hand searching for his beneath the duvet.

Harold's fingers threaded through his. They braided together the way you braid lavender stems when you tie them to dry tight, fragrant, inseparable.

Patrick returned the pressure. His pulse was steady.

He listened to the faint *tick* of the sap releasing its perfume into the room. It was an echo of summer caught inside the London night. It was a promise.

What was planted late could still survive the frost. It could still perfume the whole house when it was time to throw open the windows and let the future in.

Chapter XVI

Threads of the Past, Fabric of the Future

The rain that had stalked London for three weeks finally tired of itself. It blew away east, out toward the estuary, leaving the city rinsed, blinking, and surprised by its own reflection.

It was the first clear Saturday of August 2012.

Patrick and Harold walked toward the monthly flea market in Ealing. They took the bus from Maida Vale, a forty-minute journey that wanted to travel backwards in time.

They went partly to buy nothing. They went partly to watch other people buy nothing. But mostly, they went to walk without umbrellas, hands free and pockets open.

The market sprawled across the church car park like a family reunion for discarded objects. It was a chaotic geography of trestle tables and damp tarpaulins. It smelled of wet tarmac, fried onions from a burger van, and the specific, musty perfume of things that have spent decades in lofts waiting for a second life.

Mismatched chairs stood in conversational circles, arguing about ergonomics. Biscuit tins that smelled of other people's grandparents were stacked in precarious towers. Vinyl records, warped into gentle smiles by the sun, sat in crates, promising songs nobody hummed anymore.

They moved slowly. Their shoulders brushed. *Scuff, step. Scuff, step.*

Patrick wore his old denim jacket. Harold wore a soft grey blazer over a t-shirt: his "weekend uniform," which was indistinguishable from his work uniform, only softer, less armoured.

Patrick stopped at a table piled with postcards. He didn't read the locations; he read the fading ink, the specific, sun-bleached cyan of skies printed in 1950. They were dog-eared views of a vanished Britain. Brighton Beach crowded with woollen swimming costumes. Long-dismantled coronation arches.

Patrick turned one over.

August 1952. The ink had faded to sepia. The message was brief as a sigh.

Wish you were here. The sea is loud tonight. -J.

Patrick bought it for fifty pence. He slipped it into his breast pocket. A small time-travel device. He would pin it above Harold's desk later, a reminder that the sea had always been loud and people had always missed one another.

Harold, meanwhile, had drifted toward a stall selling "Bric-a-Brac and Curios."

He was examining a box of old fountain pens.

He picked one up. It was a black and gold Parker Duofold from the 1940s. The barrel was slightly dented, like the bell of a well-loved trumpet.

Harold uncapped it. He pressed the nib gently against the pad of his thumb. He did it with the concentration of a violinist gauging the tension of a bow: checking for flex, for scratch, for soul.

"It's a broad nib," the stallholder said. She was a woman with lilac hair and a laugh that sounded like dropping crockery. "Good for signatures. Bad for shopping lists."

Harold smiled.

"I don't make shopping lists anymore. I have people for that."

He looked at Patrick, who was wandering over.

"He means me," Patrick said to the woman. "I am 'people'."

"I'll take it," Harold said.

"I'll throw the ink in for free," the woman said, winking at Patrick. She handed Harold a bottle of Quink Blue-Black. "For love letters. Or ransom notes. Whichever comes first."

Harold paid without correcting her. His cheeks warmed in the cool air. He slipped the pen into his inside pocket, next to his heart.

They took their finds to the coffee van parked near the church gates.

They accepted cardboard cups that burned their palms. They sat on a low brick wall where the ivy had given up trying to stay green and had turned a decorative russet.

Steam rose between them like polite ghosts.

Harold blew on his coffee. He watched a family arguing over a second-hand lamp.

"I used to hate Saturdays," Harold said suddenly.

"Why?"

"The performance. When I was married. The shopping lists. The swimming lessons. The frantic attempt to cram 'leisure' into forty-eight hours. It felt like a job I wasn't qualified for."

"And now?" Patrick asked.

Harold looked at the sky. It was a pale, washed-out blue.

"Now they feel like a surplus," Harold said. "Like reaching into the pocket of last winter's coat and finding a five-pound note you didn't know you had. It's unearned wealth."

Patrick laughed. The sound startled a pigeon that had been eyeing his boots with larceny in its heart.

"We should celebrate surplus more often," Patrick said. "It is the only economics I understand."

They finished their coffee. They wandered on.

They passed trays of tarnished cutlery: spoons that had stirred a thousand cups of tea. They passed a man selling nothing but brass doorknobs, polished to the colour of sunrise, waiting for doors that no longer opened.

Near the edge of the market, tucked into the shadow of the church wall, was a stall displaying photograph albums.

They were leather-bound, cracked, peeling. Their pages were fanned open like the wings of exhausted birds.

One album lay open on top of a box.

Wedding. June 1963.

The bride's dress was wide enough to house a village. The groom looked terrified.

Patrick turned a page.

He stopped.

In the corner of a group shot—a formal family portrait arranged on a lawn—stood a boy.

He was ten years old. His hair was slicked back with Brylcreem. His tie was crooked.

He was looking at the camera with an expression of deep, secret amusement.

He had Harold's mouth.

He had Harold's uncertain, guarded smile.

Patrick froze.

"Harry," Patrick whispered.

Harold was looking at a set of silver thimbles.

"What?"

"Look."

Harold turned. He looked down at the album.

He stared. The noise of the market faded. The smell of fried onions vanished.

"That's Arthur," Harold said, pointing to a tall man in the back row. "My father. He looks... young."

"No," Patrick said. "The boy. Next to him."

Harold looked at the boy.

His breath hitched. *Hhh.*

"That... that's not me," Harold said. "The date is wrong. It is 1963."

"I know it isn't you," Patrick said. "But it is you."

Harold leaned closer. He touched the glossy surface of the photo.

"That is David," Harold whispered. "My uncle. Arthur's brother."

The stallholder, a man in a flat cap smoking a roll-up cigarette, leaned over the table.

"Whole box from a house clearance in Hanwell," the man said. "Sad business. No next of kin. The family name began with C. Carrington, I think. Are you related?"

Harold looked up. His face was pale.

"Yes," Harold said. "I am."

"Five quid for the lot," the man said. "I was going to bin them. Damp got to the spines."

Harold fumbled for his wallet. His hands were shaking.

They bought the album. They wrapped it in a blue plastic carrier bag that had once held oranges. They carried it home like a salvaged treasure.

Back at the flat in Maida Vale, the light had changed.

The late afternoon sun slanted through the sash windows, drawing stripes of gold and dust across the living room rug.

They sat on the rug.

Patrick made tea: Earl Grey, hot, comforting.

Harold sat cross-legged with the album on his knees. He turned the pages slowly. He oversaw them as if they were evidence in a capital case where the verdict had already been overturned, but the truth was still missing.

Page 1: David at ten. Holding a cricket bat, looking bored.

Page 4: David at eighteen. Naval uniform. Looking handsome, but the smile didn't reach his eyes.

Page 10: David at twenty-five. Cutting a cake with a woman whose face was turned away.

The narrative of a life. But it was full of holes.

Harold stopped at the final photograph.

It was loose at the back of the album.

It showed David on a bicycle. He was by the Thames, somewhere near Richmond. He was wearing a white shirt, the sleeves rolled up.

He was smiling. A real smile. Wide, unguarded, joyous.

He was looking at whoever held the camera with a look of pure, unadulterated love.

The river was wide behind him. It looked like a future he would never reach.

"He died in 1971," Harold said quietly. "Two years before I was born. A car crash. Or so they said."

Patrick sat beside him. He rested a warm palm against Harold's back.

"Arthur never spoke of him," Harold said. "Not once. There were no pictures in our house. It was as if he had never existed."

"Grief filed him under 'Closed'," Patrick said softly. "Arthur liked his drawers shut tight. Some drawers stay shut until someone else opens them."

Harold looked at the photo of the boy on the bicycle.

"He looks like he is escaping," Harold said. "He looks like he is trying to pedal away from the family."

"Perhaps he did," Patrick said. "Perhaps that is why Arthur erased him. Because David got away. Even if it was brief."

Harold ran his thumb over the face of the uncle he never knew.

"He looks like us," Harold whispered.

They made dinner.

Pasta again. Because grief likes familiarity. It likes carbohydrates and routine.

They spread the album open on the table between the saltshaker and the bottle of red wine.

They ate in silence, watching the faces of ghosts.

After the second glass of wine, Harold stood up.

He went to his jacket pocket. He retrieved the new pen: the black and gold Parker.

He fetched the bottle of Quink Blue-Black ink.

He sat back down.

He filled the pen. *Squeak-slurp.*

He wiped the nib with a napkin.

He opened the album to the inside cover. The paper was thick, creamy, yellowed by time.

He began to write.

His handwriting was the same as it had been at ten years old: careful, slanted, architectural. But now, it had a flow.

David Carrington, 1942 - 1971. Remembered by his nephew, Harold. Who finally found him. August 2012.

The ink shone, wet and dark. Blue-black. Like a bruise. Like the river at night.

Patrick watched the ink dry.

Then, he took the pen from Harold's hand.

He added beneath it, in his own sloping, artist's scrawl:

And by Patrick Evans. Who knows how pictures can keep someone breathing.

They closed the album.

They placed it on the lowest bookshelf, wedged between a guidebook to

Cornwall and a biography of J.M.W. Turner. They let the evening settle around it like dust that had waited decades to land.

Later, the flat grew dark.

The hum of the city dropped to a lullaby. The traffic on the Westway became a background rumble.

Harold couldn't sleep.

He got up. He went back to the living room.

He opened the album again.

He tore a blank page from the back. The paper made a tearing sound that seemed too loud in the quiet room.

He sat at the table. He picked up the pen.

He wrote a letter he had never been taught how to compose. A letter to a ghost.

Dear David,

I never knew you. But I know the shape of your smile because it lives in my mirror. I see it when I shave.

I used to think families were straight lines drawn by someone with a ruler. A family tree. Father to son. Point A to Point B.

It turns out they are threads. Some are cut. Some are knotted. Some are picked up years later by hands you never held.

I am holding one now.

It leads to a kitchen in Ealing. It leads to a man who paints oceans on bus tickets. It leads to Saturdays that feel like a surplus.

I suspect you knew about surplus. I suspect you knew about the cost of trying to fit a curve into a straight line.

If you are listening, know that the river behind you is still wide. But the bicycle is still moving. I am pedalling. I am keeping up the momentum.

Love,

Your nephew, Harry.

He folded the letter. He slipped it inside the album, pressing it between the pages like a pressed flower.

He closed the cover.

Patrick was standing in the doorway. He was holding two mugs of cocoa. He had seen the movement. He understood.

He set the mugs on the table. He sat on the arm of Harold's chair.

He wrapped his arm around Harold's shoulders.

Harold rested his head against Patrick's side.

"Do you think he was gay?" Harold whispered. "Is that why Arthur erased him?"

"I think so," Patrick said. "Or he just wanted to be something Arthur couldn't understand. An artist. A dreamer. A man who rode a bicycle with his tie undone."

"I am glad we found him."

"He was waiting to be found."

Outside, a police siren doppler away. *Nee-naw.*

Somewhere else, a dog barked once.

Inside, the two men sat shoulder to shoulder. The album lay heavy on the table like a promise that had finally found its weight.

The city continued its nocturnal rehearsal of neon and brake lights. But inside the flat, the air was still. It was scented with ink, cocoa, and the faint, sweet ghost of a 1960s wedding cake.

When they went to bed, they left the album on the coffee table.

Spine cracked. Pages breathing.

In the dark, beneath the heavy oatmeal duvet, Harold whispered.

"I think he would have liked you, Pat."

Patrick squeezed Harold's hand.

"He already does," Patrick replied. "He is in the room."

They slept then. Hands loosely clasped.

In the living room, the photograph album remained open to the page where a boy on a bicycle smiled at a future he couldn't reach.

But now, beneath the photo, two new lines of wet ink kept him pedalling.

Kept him moving.

Kept him alive inside the bright, small room that smelled of cocoa and possibility and the quiet, stubborn persistence of being seen.

Chapter XVII

The Language of Silence

Sunday arrived grey and with bated breath.

The city outside their Maida Vale flat was reduced to a charcoal smudge of rooftops, wet slate, and a drizzle so fine it looked like fog suspended in a glass jar.

Patrick woke first. His head was thick with the residue of last night's dreams: disjointed images of ink refusing to dry, of bicycles pedalling through a fog that tasted of a 1960s wedding cake, of a river flowing backward against the tide.

He lay still for a moment, listening. The flat was silent, save for the soft, rhythmic puff of Harold's breathing beside him.

Patrick slipped out of bed. He walked to the kitchen. He stood at the sink, watching the rain crawl down the windowpane like slow, methodical caterpillars. *Slide. Stop. Slide.*

The photograph album lay on the coffee table where they had left it the night before. Its spine was cracked. Its pages breathed softly in the warm air, exhaling the secrets they had kept for forty years.

Patrick made coffee. He made it in silence, flinching at the *click* of the spoon against the ceramic mug.

He carried it to the studio corner. It was just the back end of the living room —an L-shaped alcove—but Patrick had claimed it. It held his easel, the north-facing window, and a radiator that rattled like a sick heart.

He taped a fresh sheet of hot-pressed paper to his drawing board.

He picked up the pen. The black and gold Parker Duofold Harold had bought at the flea market.

He did not dip it in ink. It was still loaded with last night's Quink Blue-Black.

He began to draw.

He did not draw the bicycle. He did not draw the river.

He drew the space between them.

He drew the negative shapes. He drew the tension of the air around the spokes.

And then, he began to write.

He used the pen to create the frame of the bicycle, but he did not use lines. He used words. Harold's letter to David. *Dear David... I never knew you...*

He wrote the words so small they were almost invisible, just a texture of blue-black ink. The crossbar was a sentence about straight lines. The handlebars were a sentence about surplus.

The wheels were empty space. White paper.

The river behind the bicycle was a single, continuous sentence stretching across the page. *I am pedalling. I am pedalling. I am pedalling.*

It was the most precise thing Patrick had ever done.

Harold appeared an hour later.

He wore his pyjama bottoms and a grey t-shirt. His hair stood up on the left side, looking like a boy who had fallen asleep in a car against the window.

He stood in the doorway of the alcove. He did not speak.

He walked up behind Patrick. He smelled of sleep and the warmth of cotton.

He looked over Patrick's shoulder.

He watched the pen move. *Scratch. Scratch.*

The only sound in the room was the nib on the paper, the occasional wheeze of the radiator, and the rain tapping against the glass like someone asking to be let in.

Patrick finished the final ripple of the river. He capped the pen. *Click.*

He took a step back.

Harold leaned in. He adjusted his glasses. He looked at the bicycle made of words.

He exhaled. It was a sound that could have been a laugh, or it could have been something breaking inside his chest.

"You drew the silence," Harold said. His voice was rough with morning.

Patrick nodded.

"Silence has edges, Harry. I just followed them."

Harold reached out. He touched the corner of the paper gently, as if it might bruise if he pressed too hard.

"It is beautiful," he whispered.

They ate breakfast without speaking.

Soft-boiled eggs. Toast cut into soldiers. The last of the marmalade Mrs. Gable had pressed into their hands months ago, the jar wrapped in newspaper.

The silence was not heavy. It did not feel like the silence of the launderette years ago, which was crowded with unspoken things.

This silence was comfortable. It fit like an overcoat that had been waiting in the hallway all winter and now, finally slipped on, fit perfectly.

Afterward, Harold cleared the table. The china clinked softly.

He placed the photograph album in the centre of the table.

He opened it to the last page. The photo of David on the bicycle.

He picked up Patrick's fountain pen.

He sat down. He uncapped it.

He wrote beneath the photograph, below Patrick's inscription. His handwriting was microscopic.

Silence is only a pause. The sentence continues.

He dated it. *12 August.* He initialled it. *H.C.*

He closed the album.

Then, he did something Patrick had never seen him do.

He pushed the album aside. He placed both palms flat on the table, splaying his fingers against the wood. He closed his eyes.

He sat like that for thirty seconds. Breathing slowly. In... out.

It was the posture of someone preparing to plunge into water they know is cold, but necessary.

When he opened his eyes, he looked at Patrick.

"I need to not speak today," Harold said.

Patrick looked at him.

"All right."

"Not because I am angry," Harold clarified. "It is just... I have no room for anything else today. My uncle. The letter. The past. All of it..."

Patrick understood. He himself had lived inside that kind of fullness. Days when language felt like a shoe two sizes too small, pinching the toes.

Patrick nodded. He poured more coffee into Harold's mug.

"Understood," Patrick said.

He touched Harold's shoulder, then turned and walked into the bedroom, leaving Harold in the quiet.

The hours unfolded like a single, uncreased sheet of paper.

They existed in parallel.

Harold sat in the armchair by the window. He had a stack of briefs for the week, but he did not mark them. He read them, staring fixedly at the clauses. He made notes in the margins that were only symbols: arrows, circles, a small star.

At midday, he stood up. He put on his coat. He walked to the corner shop.

He walked back. He bought nothing. The act of walking itself was the purchase. He needed the rhythm of his feet on the pavement.

Patrick painted in the bedroom. The light was softer there.

He worked on a series of small watercolours, the size of postcards.

He painted the space between two pillows on the unmade bed.

He painted the negative shape where Harold's hand had rested on the kitchen counter.

He painted the outline of a bicycle made entirely of sky blue, dissolving into the white of the paper.

They moved around one another in the flat. A choreography of intimacy.

When Harold made tea, he made a cup for Patrick and left it silently beside the easel. Patrick squeezed Harold's hand in thanks. Without words.

At four o'clock, the rain stopped.

The clouds lifted like a heavy velvet curtain being hauled into the rafters of the sky. They revealed a pale, washed-out blue that looked almost white.

Harold appeared in the bedroom doorway.

He touched Patrick's shoulder. He pointed toward the door.

Let's go.

They went out.

They walked to Warwick Avenue station. They took the Underground.

The train carriage was quiet. The lethargy of Sunday afternoon. They sat side by side, their knees touching. They did not read. They just watched the black tunnel glide by.

At Ealing Broadway, they surfaced.

The streets smelled of wet pavement and lilac.

They walked past the old high street. Past the ghosts of the shops that used to be there.

They walked toward the park.

They reached the stream.

The place where the fallen horse chestnut had once laid—the tree they had crossed in 1984—was gone. The trunk had rotted away or had been removed by the council years ago.

In its place was a metal footbridge. It was painted a municipal green. It had handrails. It was safe. It was sensible.

They walked onto the bridge. Their footsteps echoed on the metal. *Clang. Clang.*

They stood in the middle.

They looked down at the water.

It moved beneath them. Brown, swollen with rain, churning over the stones.

It was the same water. Or it was the water that had replaced the water. It carried the memory of their reflections from twenty-five years ago.

Two boys. Balancing. Terrified. Holding hands.

Now, they were two men. Older. Broader. Standing on solid metal.

Harold reached into his pocket.

He pulled out the black and gold fountain pen.

He uncapped it.

He leaned over the railing.

On the flat, green-painted metal of the handrail, he wrote.

The ink was a dark blue-black against the green enamel.

H.C. + P.E.

He paused.

Then he wrote:

the sentence continues.

The ink beaded on the cold metal. Then it caught. Then, slowly, in the biting air, it began to dry.

They watched it.

They watched it until it was permanent. Until the stillness felt complete. Until the sky over Ealing had faded to a soft pearl grey that suggested night without insisting upon it.

Harold capped the pen. He tucked it back into his pocket.

He looked at Patrick.

He smiled. A small, tired, and genuine smile.

They walked home in that quiet.

Hands in pockets. Shoulders occasionally brushing.

The city folded around them like a book.

Inside the flat, the spell held.

They made tea. They fed the cat.

Patrick took the small watercolours he had painted that afternoon. He stuck them to the living room wall with Blu-Tack that smelled of primary school.

They stepped back. They inspected the silence of the day made visible.

The pillows. The handprint. The bicycle of sky.

They felt the future settle upon their shoulders. It was soft as dust. It was no longer heavy.

Later, in bed, the darkness was absolute.

Harold rolled onto his side. He found Patrick's hand beneath the duvet.

He broke the silence.

"I spoke to David today," Harold whispered.

Patrick turned his head on the pillow.

"And what did he say?"

"He said that silence is not the end. It is only a pause between pedals," Harold said. "He said, 'Keep going, Harry. Keep up the momentum.'"

Patrick squeezed his hand.

"Then we keep going."

"Yes."

They slept then. Hands loosely clasped.

Outside, the city continued its nocturnal rehearsal. Sirens. Brake lights. The Piccadilly line rumbling deep below.

Inside, the album remained closed on the coffee table. The ink was dry. The silence was complete.

The sentence—inked by two hands, spanned by a red thread, and spoken in the language of a Sunday stillness—was waiting for the morning to begin again.

Chapter XVIII

The Embrace of London

Sunday's silence dried into a thin, translucent skin.

Monday arrived bright and restless. The city shook the rain from its coat like a dog fresh out of the Serpentine: wet, vigorous, and ready to run.

It was September 2012.

Patrick woke first.

He made the coffee. He carried his mug to the living room windowsill.

The lavender cuttings they had taken from Mrs. Gable's garden were beginning to root in their mismatched jars. Pale, white threads hung in the water, searching for purchase, looking for somewhere to land.

Behind him, in the bedroom, Harold's breathing steadied. It was no longer the heavy sleep of exhaustion. It was the slow, satisfied rhythm of dreams that had decided to stay.

The kettle clicked off. *Click.*

A siren doppler away down the Westway. *Nee-naw.*

The day declared itself open for business.

They left the flat together just after nine.

Their shoulders brushed in the hallway. *Bump.* It was a habit now. A calibration of proximity that required no consultation.

Harold carried his leather satchel. It was full of briefs he would later discover he didn't need.

Patrick carried a sketchbook smaller than his palm. He had a pencil sharpened to surgical precision tucked behind his ear.

They walked to the corner of the Crescent.

"Don't be late," Patrick said.

"I am never late," Harold said. "I am just... temporarily optimistic."

They parted ways.

Harold turned left toward Warwick Avenue Underground station. Patrick turned right toward the canal and the river beyond.

Every movement was economical. Rehearsed. It was the small, precise choreography of two people who have learned the exact shape of each other's absence, and who know the separation is only temporary.

Patrick walked.

He walked the way he painted: without a destination, waiting for something to announce itself as worth keeping.

He walked along the canal to Little Venice, then down toward the river.

Along the Embankment, the barges motored upstream. Their wakes fanned out behind them like apologies.

He stopped beneath a plane tree. It was older than the benches bolted down around it. Its bark was peeling in camouflage patches of grey and cream.

Patrick opened the small sketchbook.

He didn't draw the tree. He didn't draw the river.

He drew the negative space between the branches.

Not the leaves. Not the sky. Just the air that allowed them both to exist. The shape of the gap.

The pencil moved without permission. *Scrape-scratch.* He watched his own hand moving the way you watch weather happen in someone else's city: with interest, but without anxiety.

Across the water, the dome of St. Paul's sat copper-green against the washed-out blue sky.

Patrick remembered drawing that dome when he was fifteen. He had sat on a wall in Ealing and declared it impossible to capture. "It's too perfect," he had told Harold. "I can't get the curve right."

He had been wrong. Nothing was impossible. Just slow.

He finished the sketch.

He tore the page from the book. The paper made a sharp ripping sound.

He folded it. *Fold. Crease. Fold.*

He made a paper boat.

He walked to the edge of the water. He leaned over the balustrade.

He dropped the boat.

It landed in the grey water. It bobbed once. Then, it began to absorb the river. It dissolved before it reached the opposite bank.

But the dissolution felt like a completion. It wasn't loss. It was release.

Harold, meanwhile, was descending into the Underground.

The satchel bumped against his hip like a small, obedient pet.

The platform smelled of electricity, wet wool, and the metallic taste of brake dust.

The train arrived. *Whoosh.*

It was packed. They read phones the way commuters used to read newspapers: the same bowed heads, the same silence, the same desperate avoidance of eye contact.

Harold found a corner. He hooked his elbow around the pole.

He opened his satchel. He pulled out the brief he had drafted the night before. *The Winchester Merger.*

He looked at the words. "Hereinafter referred to as..."

The words blurred.

He closed the file.

Instead, he watched the reflections in the window opposite.

Faces superimposed over black tunnels. Faces superimposed over cables. Faces superimposed over nothing.

His own face floated among them.

He looked older. The lines around his mouth were deeper. But he looked softer at the edges.

He was wearing the grey cashmere scarf: the one Patrick had given him years ago, the one that smelled of cedar and time. It was bright against his corporate overcoat.

He looked, he realized, like a man who had remembered mid-journey where he was going.

At Holborn, he surfaced.

He walked through the glass doors of his Chambers.

The security guard nodded. "Morning, Mr. Carrington."

"Morning, Frank."

Harold went to his office. He set the brief aside on the mahogany desk.

He pulled out the black and gold fountain pen.

He pulled out a blank sheet of thick, cream-coloured headed paper.

He didn't write a contract. He didn't write a clause.

He wrote a list.

* Ferry at dawn, fog low enough to taste.
* Lavander cutting taking root on a windowsill.
* The Exact weight of a hand on my shoulder when words fail.
* David's bicycle, still pedalling in the dark.
* Paper boats that dissolve before reaching the far bank.
* The space between the leaves that allows both to exist.

He looked at the list.

It wasn't poetry. It wasn't law. It was evidence.

He dated the page. *September 2012.* He initialled it. *H.C.*

He slipped it into the bottom drawer: the drawer that had once held only amendments, affidavits, and secrets.

Then, he stood up.

He put his coat on.

He walked out to the reception desk.

"I will be out for the rest of the day, Maria," he told the secretary.

"Is everything all right, sir?"

"Yes," Harold said. "Everything is exactly right."

They met at Borough Market just after midday.

They were drawn by hunger and by the unspoken agreement that lunch tasted better when bought from people who knew their cows' names.

Harold arrived carrying a paper bag that smelled of cardamom and butter.

Patrick arrived carrying two apples the colour of a bruised sunset and a small painting wrapped in brown paper.

They found a space against a brick wall warmed by the weak autumn sun.

They ate without ceremony. They tore the croissants. They bit into the apples. The juice ran down their wrists.

Patrick wiped his mouth with the back of his hand.

"Here," Patrick said.

He handed Harold the small brown paper parcel.

Harold wiped his hands on a napkin. He unwrapped it.

It was a painting. Small. The size of a postcard.

It was an indigo wash: deep, dark blue.

But stitched through the thick watercolour paper was a single red thread.

It went in one side and out the other. It was tied in a loose loop in the centre.

Harold held it up to the light. The thread cast a shadow on the paper. It looked exactly like a bridge.

"For your desk," Patrick said. "So, you don't forget why we fix things. Sometimes you must stitch things back together."

Harold's throat closed. He touched the thread.

"Thank you," he whispered.

He slipped the painting into the inside pocket of his overcoat. It sat next to his heart: a heart that had begun to beat in sentences instead of clauses.

They walked after they ate.

They let the crowd push them wherever it wanted.

The stalls offered olives the size of coins. Cheese veined like maps of undiscovered countries. Bread still steaming in the crisp air.

They bought nothing else. They were content to carry what they already held.

Eventually, they ended up on the South Bank.

The benches were full of tourists eating sandwiches wrapped in foil that flashed like mirrors in the sun. *Flash. Flash.*

Harold and Patrick sat on a low wall. Their knees pointed toward the water.

They watched the city perform its daily miracle: standing upright while moving exceedingly fast.

Harold spoke first.

"I used to think London was a contract," he said. "Non-negotiable terms. Breach punishable by loneliness. Specific performance."

Patrick considered this. He watched a barge moving sluggishly downriver.

"And now?"

"Now," Harold said, "it's a sketch. You draw the line. You rub it out. You draw it again. The paper holds the ghost of the mistake, but the ghost doesn't mind. The ghost adds texture."

Across the river, a red bus pulled away from a stop. It was the colour of the thread in Harold's pocket.

They watched it go.

Neither mentioned the scarf hanging by the door at home, the one that now carried the faint scent of lavender instead of cedar.

A boat sounded its horn. *Blaaart.* Low and forgiving.

They stood up. They brushed the crumbs from their coats.

They began the slow walk home.

They didn't hold hands. The pavement was too crowded. The day was too public.

But their shadows overlapped on the stone.

One long, dark shape stretching out ahead of them. Turning corners as one. Pausing when they paused. Continuing when they continued.

At the flat, they took off their shoes.

They filled the kettle.

Patrick opened the sash windows to let in the evening perfume of the city. Diesel. River mud. The last lilacs from the garden down the street.

Harold took the small painting from his pocket.

He propped it against the base of the lamp on the side table.

The light hit the red thread. It cast its bridge across the white wall behind it.

They stepped back.

They surveyed the room.

It held lavender cuttings taking root in water.

It held a photograph album of a lost uncle.

It held a list that refused to be a contract.

It held a painting of a bicycle made of words.

They felt the future settling. It was soft as dust. It covered every surface.

Later, in bed, the lights were out.

Harold turned to Patrick in the dark.

"I crossed an ocean," Harold whispered. "But today, I crossed the river."

Patrick smiled. Harold could hear the smile in his voice.

"Same water, Harry. Different direction."

They slept then.

Hands loosely clasped beneath the duvet.

Outside, London continued its nocturnal rehearsal. Lights. Brakes. The small, determined lives refusing to be quiet.

Inside, the city was briefly still.

Two men.

A bridge of red thread.

A room that had learned to hold them without asking for anything more than the ordinary miracle of waking up and choosing, again, to stay.

Chapter XIX

The Unfolding Chapters

Time, in the end, became a silent collaborator.

It was no longer the enemy that slammed doors or stole parents. It was no longer the frantic railway station clock nor the billable hour. It became a travelling companion. A quiet man who handed them a paintbrush and said, "Keep going. The canvas is still wet."

The seasons turned in that soft, ordinary way that feels fast in the moment but slow in memory.

There were winters that smelled of radiator steam, damp wool, and Harold's cedar cologne. There were springs when the plane trees along the canal coughed up a lime-green fuzz that clung to their coats, and Patrick mixed the exact shade of "New Leaf Green" on a palette chipped at the edges.

There were summers of night buses with the windows rolled down, the air tasting of diesel and river breath, hot and alive. There were autumns that arrived like a sigh of relief, dropping leaves the colour of wedding confetti into the gutters outside the pubs they now called their locals.

They aged in increments small enough to be missed daily, but undeniable in the aggregate.

Patrick noticed the first silver hair at Harold's temple on a Tuesday evening in the lamplight. He didn't say anything; he just reached out and touched it. Harold flinched, then leaned into the touch.

Harold noticed the faint map of lines deepening around Patrick's eyes: crow's feet from squinting at horizons. He traced them with a thumb at dawn, as if memorizing a new geography he would have to navigate.

Their bodies learned each other's rhythms the way sailors learn the weather: by skin, by breath, by the small creak of bones settling after a long walk home.

Arthritis visited. It stayed for coffee. It left again, then returned for the weekend.

Prescriptions gathered in the bathroom cabinet like shy guests. Statins. Beta-blockers. Vitamin D. They took the pills with the same ceremony with which they drank tea: the kettle, the mug, the glass of water, the quiet acceptance that maintenance is its own form of devotion.

Harold's career shifted gears.

The law firm granted him full partnership, but he negotiated a new contract. He worked three-day weeks. He became "Of Counsel."

The juniors called him "The Silent Oracle." They brought him the messy cases, the ones involving families and emotions, because they knew he could find the structure in the chaos.

They never knew that the cases he turned down—the massive corporate mergers, the hostile takeovers—were the ones that would have kept him away from the studio at 4:00 p.m.

At 4:00 p.m., Harold went home. He took off his tie. He put on an old jumper.

He walked into the spare room.

Patrick handed him a brush.

"Paint the negative space," Patrick would say. "Paint the air between my fingers."

Harold painted badly. He painted with joy. He painted with the enthusiasm of a man who has spent fifty years colouring inside the lines and has finally been given permission to scribble.

The colours ran. The perspective tilted. Apples looked like pears. Bridges looked as though they would collapse under the weight of a feather.

"It is expressionist," Patrick declared, pinning a crooked watercolour of the cat to the hallway wall.

"It is a disaster," Harold beamed.

They hung the results in the hallway anyway. Misshapen fruit. Lavender fields that looked like bruises. A portrait of Patrick that resembled a storm cloud.

Visitors—friends who had become family, family who had become friends—pretended to admire them.

"It has... energy," Nek said, visiting from New York with her new wife.

"It has Harold," Patrick corrected. "That is enough."

Patrick's exhibitions grew smaller, but brighter.

Elena retired to a villa in Tuscany. Her assistant, a sharp young man named Julian who wore impeccable suits, took over the gallery.

"We need a retrospective," Julian insisted. "Patrick Evans: Thirty Years of

Light."

Patrick agreed, but on one condition.

"The final room," Patrick said, "will be a collaboration."

Julian hesitated.

"A collaboration with whom?"

"With H. Carrington. Amateur. Unapologetic."

The opening was held on a Thursday evening in late October 2018. The light was kind: golden and low.

They didn't serve champagne. They served cheap red wine in plastic cups, the kind that stains your teeth. They played Nina Simone because the gallery speakers refused to play anything faster.

Harold wore the grey cashmere scarf. It was soft as dust now, fraying at the ends, but it stood out against his velvet blazer.

Patrick wore paint on his cuffs—he had stopped trying to scrub it off for public appearances—and the same crooked smile he had worn at nineteen. Only now, the smile was deeper. It was like a river that had learned its course and stopped fighting the banks.

The critics walked through the main rooms. They nodded at the Indigo Nights. They murmured over the Red Thread series.

Then they reached the final room.

It was hung with Harold's watercolours. The crooked dog. The tilting bridge. The bruised lavender.

And beside each one, Patrick had painted a response: a hyper-realistic study of the same subject, honouring Harold's clumsy vision with his own masterful technique.

The critics called the pairing "a quiet revolution against perfection."

Patrick stood in the corner, holding Harold's hand.

"I call it marriage," Patrick whispered.

They travelled. But they travelled light.

No more oceans. No more red-eye flights to Heathrow.

They took slow trains. They wandered through English counties whose names they mispronounced on purpose. Leominster. Mousehole.

They stayed in B&Bs where the landlady left shortbread on the pillow and asked no questions about why two men in their late fifties wanted the double room with a view.

They walked coastal paths in Cornwall. Harold kept smooth stones in his pockets: grey, white, speckled. His coat pockets filled with geology.

Patrick sketched crumbling cliffs in miniature in the margins of the page.

They sent postcards.

Not to Olivia, her address was now a memory.

They sent them to Thomas, who lived in Los Angeles making documentaries. They sent them to Sarah, who was an architect in Manchester.

View of the lighthouse. Weather kind. Company better. Home soon. P & H.

Thomas kept them. He lined them up on his mantelpiece in Laurel Canyon. A paper skyline of his father's happiness.

Illness arrived. As it does. Uninvited, but expected.

It was the winter of 2023.

Harold's heart murmured. Then it stuttered. Then, on a Tuesday morning while making toast, it decided to pause.

The ambulance ride was a blur of blue lights and wet pavement.

They sat in the cardiology ward for three days.

Harold required scaffolding. Wire. Stents. Science.

Patrick sat in the plastic chair beside the bed. He didn't paint. He couldn't hold the brush steady.

He played gin rummy with Harold. They used a deck of cards borrowed from a woman in the next bed who taught them how to cheat gracefully.

"I am winning," Harold whispered, his voice groggy from the anaesthetic.

"You are cheating," Patrick said, holding Harold's hand so tightly his knuckles were white.

"It is the same thing."

Harold slept.

Patrick looked out the window. He memorized the view. The car park roofs. A sliver of the Thames. The sky above it trying to decide on blue but settling for grey.

When they wheeled Harold back from the procedure, he looked pale. Greyer than the Thames.

He opened his eyes. He looked at Patrick.

"Have you mixed a warmer sky on the left?" Harold asked.

Patrick nodded. He pressed his forehead against Harold's hand. He knew, with a terrifying clarity, that the conversation would never again be about trivia. Every sentence was now a negotiation with time.

They sold the Maida Vale flat eventually.

The stairs were too much. The city was too loud.

They bought a small house in Ealing.

It was not Number 42. It was not Number 44. It was a cottage near the common, with a garden that had forgotten it was a garden and believed itself a meadow.

They let it grow.

Knee-high grass. Poppies spilling over the path like drunken dancers. Lavender spreading like a rumour, taking over the flowerbeds.

They installed a wooden bench beneath the apple tree.

They sat there most evenings.

Reading. Not reading. Watching the aeroplanes blink across the sky on their way to Heathrow, on their way to somewhere faster.

They held hands without thinking. Fingers threaded together. Sentences too long for a single line.

One autumn, when the leaves were the colour of burnt caramel and the air smelled of school uniforms and distant bonfires, Harold closed his law books for good.

He stacked them in the hallway. *Tort Law. Contract Theory. The Nature of Obligations.*

"I am done," Harold announced.

He spent his Tuesdays learning pottery at the local community centre.

The wheel spattered clay across his cuffs. Across the ceiling. Across Patrick's white hair when he leaned in too close to offer advice.

"It is the centring," Harold would insist, wrestling with a lump of grey mud.

"It is eccentric," Patrick would laugh, wiping clay from his cheek.

The pots came out crooked. Thick-walled. Heavy. They were always the same soft grey as the river at dawn.

They drank coffee from them anyway. Their lips tasted of earth and effort and the stubborn refusal to be perfect.

Patrick's final exhibition opened on a Thursday in October.

He was seventy-two years old.

The gallery was a pop-up space in Ealing: an old butcher's shop. The tiles were still white. The meat hooks had been removed, but the memory of them remained.

Patrick hung twenty paintings.

Harold reading. Harold asleep in the chair. Harold painting badly. The garden refusing to be tidy. The cat refusing to sit still.

The final canvas was larger than the rest.

It was an Indigo Night. Deep. Dark. Infinite.

Bisected by a single Red Thread.

The thread dipped and rose. It looped. It tangled. And finally, in the centre of the canvas, it knotted itself into a loose, comfortable bow.

Beneath it, in lettering too small to read without stepping close, Patrick had written the title.

We were never the hero of this story. We were the thread that refused to break. Thank you for watching us stay.

People came. Neighbours. Thomas and his husband. Sarah and her children. Mrs. Gable's granddaughter.

They drank the wine. They ate the cheese (artisan, naturally).

At nine o'clock, Patrick turned the sign on the door to *Closed.*

He dimmed the lights.

He stood beside Harold in front of the last painting.

Harold leaned on a walking stick now. Patrick's hands trembled slightly.

They didn't say anything for a long time.

Then, Harold slipped his arm around Patrick's waist. It was the gesture of closing a book you know you will never read again because you have memorized every word.

"Ready to go home?" Harold asked.

"Yes," Patrick said. "I am ready."

They stepped out into the night.

They walked home through streets that smelled of wet leaves and the very last of the summer heat.

Harold wore the grey scarf. It was old now, but bright against the dark.

The thread was finally visible. It was finally enough.

Years later, when visitors asked how long they had been together, they didn't give a number.

They didn't say "forty years" or "fifty years." They didn't speak of the gap, or the silence, or the ocean.

They answered in unison, their voices rough with age but steady with certainty:

"Long enough."

"Long enough to know when the other doesn't need to speak."

"And to call this home."

Epilogue

The Unfolding Silence

The house near St. Albans Avenue settles into the night.

It settles the way an old dog lowers itself onto a familiar rug: with aching bones, steady breath, but still alert to every footstep on the pavement outside. It is a house that has memorized the rhythm of its occupants. It knows which floorboards creak (the third one on the landing). It knows which window rattles when the planes from Heathrow bank low (the sash in the spare room).

Inside, the light is failing.

It is a bruised, violet light: the colour of a healing bruise, or of a day deciding to forgive itself for the rain.

On the windowsill, the lavender cuttings Patrick took from Mrs. Gable's garden decades ago are now ancient, woody bushes in the garden below, but a fresh sprig wilts gently in a jam jar on the ledge.

The cat—a sleek black creature they named Thread—sleeps across the warm spine of a closed photograph album. Its tail twitches. It dreams of birds it is too slow to catch.

Two mugs of coffee are cooling on the side table. They are mismatched. One is delicate china, a survivor from Patrick's mother's set. The other is a thick, crooked mug Harold threw during his pottery phase, glazed the colour of the Thames at low tide.

The rims are touched by lips that have said everything, and nothing, today.

8:00 A.M.

The day had begun the way they all do now: slowly.

Patrick woke first. He lay in bed, listening to the house breathe.

He felt the stiffness in his knuckles. Arthritis is a tenant that refuses to pay rent; it simply takes up space in the joints, demanding attention. Patrick flexed his hand. Open. Close. The movement was gritty, like sand in a bearing.

Beside him, Harold was a mound of stillness beneath the heavy duvet. Harold breathed with a slight wheeze now, a souvenir from the heart surgery years ago. *Hhh-shhh. Hhh-shhh.*

Patrick watched him. He watched the way the morning light, filtering through the oatmeal curtains, caught the silver in Harold's stubble. The map of lines around Harold's eyes was deep, a topography of worry and laughter that Patrick knew better than his own face.

Harold stirred. One eye opened. It was clouded, a greyish blue.

"You are staring," Harold croaked.

"I am studying," Patrick corrected. "The light is good."

"The light is cruel. It highlights the erosion."

"It is not erosion, Harry. It is texture."

They got up in stages. The swinging of legs over the side of the bed. The pause to let blood pressure settle. The search for slippers.

They went downstairs. The stairs were a negotiation. Patrick went first, gripping the banister. Harold followed, carrying his walking stick: a beautiful piece of polished ash Patrick had carved for him.

In the kitchen, they performed the breakfast ballet.

Harold filled the kettle. Patrick measured the tea. They moved around one another without colliding; a choreography perfected over forty years.

They sat at the table. They looked out at the garden.

The garden had forgotten it was a garden. It believed itself a meadow. The grass was knee-high, swaying in the wind. The apple tree was gnarled, dropping fruit that no one picked up, leaving it for the foxes.

"We should get a gardener," Harold said. He said this every morning.

"We like it wild," Patrick replied. He replied this every morning.

"It is untidy. It lacks structure."

"It has narrative," Patrick said. "Look at the poppies. They are rioting."

Harold smiled into his tea.

"You always did prefer a riot to a rule."

11:00 A.M.

Mid-morning. Archive hour.

They sat in the living room. The sun had moved around the house, warming the rug.

Harold opened the sideboard drawer. It was the "Museum Drawer."

He pulled out the artifacts.

The rusted tin of *Roses* chocolates.

The black and gold Parker fountain pen (the nib now bent).

Uncle David's postcard (*The sea is loud tonight*).

The grey cashmere scarf, now so thin it was almost translucent, folded in tissue paper like a holy relic.

Harold put on his reading glasses. They settled on the tip of his nose.

He picked up the pen. He held it in his hand, weighing it.

"I was thinking about the bridge today," Harold said.

"Which bridge?"

"The one in the park. Where I wrote the equation. H.C. + P.E."

"I remember."

"I wonder if it is still there," Harold said. "Or if the council painted over it."

"The council paints over everything eventually," Patrick said. "That is their job. Keeping things tidy."

"But the ink was waterproof," Harold insisted. "Quink Blue-Black. Permanent."

Patrick picked up his sketchbook. He wasn't drawing. He was just holding the stick of charcoal, feeling the texture.

"It doesn't matter if it is on the bridge, Harry. It is in the book."

Harold nodded. He opened the photograph album from beneath the sleeping cat.

He turned the pages.

David on the bicycle.

Patrick at nineteen, paint in his hair.

Harold at forty, looking terrified in a tuxedo.

The two of them in Provincetown, squinting into the fog.

"We looked young," Harold said.

"We were young."

"I didn't feel young. I felt... terrified. I felt like I was holding my breath."

Patrick reached out. He covered Harold's hand with his own. His skin was paper-thin, mottled with age. Harold's hand was cool, the veins prominent blue cords.

"You exhaled," Patrick said. "Eventually."

"Yes. I did."

Harold closed the book.

"Did we build enough, Pat?" Harold asked suddenly. "I look at the cases I settled. The contracts. It is all paper. It is all filed away in a basement somewhere."

Patrick looked around the room. He looked at the paintings on the wall. He looked at the lavender on the windowsill.

"We built a world," Patrick said. "Inside a house in Ealing. It is small. But it is complete."

2:00 P.M.

The afternoon nap.

It was no longer a choice. It was a biological imperative. The battery was running low.

Harold fell asleep in the armchair, his mouth slightly open, the biography of some long-dead politician slipping from his fingers.

Patrick did not sleep. He sat on the sofa, watching Harold.

He thought about Time.

Time, that old collaborator. It keeps its own ledger.

It had taken what it needed. It had taken the speed from their legs. It had taken the certainty from their hands. It had taken the elasticity of youth, the way skin bounces back.

But what it left behind was quieter. And, more valuable.

It left an allowance. Measured in spoonfuls of light at dawn. Measured in the creak of a knee coming down a staircase. Measured in the way a hand still finds a hand across a duvet in the middle of the night, even when the dark has forgotten the shape of them.

Patrick picked up a pencil.

He sketched Harold sleeping.

He drew the slackness of the jaw. The thinness of the hair. The vulnerability of the throat.

He didn't try to make him beautiful. He tried to make him true.

This is the man who crossed the ocean. This is the man who bought the black and gold pen. This is the man who learned to live without straight lines.

Patrick finished the sketch. He wrote the date at the bottom. *November 2045*.

He closed the book.

6:00 P.M.

Upstairs, the studio lamp burns.

Patrick climbed the stairs slowly. *One. Two.* Breath. *Three. Four.*

He entered the spare room.

The easel stood in the centre.

One final canvas waited.

It was an Indigo Night.

He had laid down the background weeks ago. A wash of deep, velvety blue. The colour of the London sky at 4:00 a.m.

The decorator's brush lay in the tray, stiff with dried paint.

But the final element—the red thread—was not painted.

The red paint was still coiled on the palette. A crusted drop of Cadmium Red.

Patrick stood before the canvas.

He picked up a fine liner brush. He dipped it into the medium. He revived the red paint.

He held the brush toward the canvas.

He looked at the indigo void.

He thought about painting the thread. Connecting the left side to the right side. Making the bridge.

His hand hovered.

Then, he lowered the brush.

He did not paint the line.

He realized, suddenly, that he didn't need to. The thread was no longer paint. It was not a symbol. It was the air in the room. It was the motes of dust dancing in the lamplight. It was the sound of Harold coughing downstairs.

To paint it would be to confine it.

He cleaned the brush. He left the indigo canvas. Empty. And full.

He switched off the lamp.

9:00 P.M.

The light switch flicks off downstairs.

The studio window reflects two figures. Smaller now. Stooped. Silhouettes against a city that has finally learned their names and is prepared, tonight, to let them keep them.

They climb the stairs to the bedroom.

"Did you lock the back door?" Harold asks. The eternal question.

"Yes, Harry."

"Did you put the cat out?"

"The cat is already on the bed. He runs the place."

They undress. The shedding of the day's clothes. The folding of the trousers. The placing of the glasses on the bedside table.

They get into bed.

The sheets are cool.

They lie on their backs.

The city outside continues its nocturnal rehearsal.

Sirens. *Nee-naw.*

Brake lights sweeping across the ceiling like red ghosts.

The soft complaint of the plane trees in the wind.

Inside, their breathing synchronizes.

In... out. In... out.

It slows. It almost stops.

Almost. But not quite.

They are not the hero of this story. They never were. Heroes conquer. Heroes win.

They did something harder. They stayed.

They are the sentence that refused to end with a full stop. They are the pause that gathered momentum. They are the thread that wore thin, fraying at the edges, but did not snap.

The book closes. The paint dries. The ferry reaches the opposite shore.

And yet the water continues. Carrying them. Carrying the bright, small wake of what they chose to build together.

Midnight.

Somewhere in Ealing, a bus turns a corner. It is the colour of childhood. Red. Bright. It vanishes into the fog.

Somewhere, a scarf lifts in a breeze that smells of cedar and river salt.

Somewhere, a paper boat dissolves before reaching the opposite shore. And that, too, is arrival. Dissolving into the thing that carries you.

In the dark, Harold's hand moves.

It travels across the duvet. A slow, trembling expedition.

It finds Patrick's hand.

Patrick's fingers open. They thread together.

Bone against bone. Pulse against pulse.

The thread knots. It slackens. It knots again.

The sentence continues.

And if you listen—really listen—you will hear it still.

Beneath the hum of the fridge. Beneath the roar of the Heathrow planes. Beneath the silence of the garden.

The low, steady hum of two hearts refusing to close the book.

The faint *click* of pedals keeping rhythm on a bicycle built for two.

The quiet vow that tomorrow will arrive ordinary and enough.

It arrives the way every love story arrives:

Unfinished.

Unpunctuated.

Unending.

Time moves on.

The thread holds.

The canvas waits.

Acknowledgments

Authoring a book is, for the most part, a solitary conversation; but guiding a story to its final pages requires a bridge built by others.

To my family: Thank you for being the first foundations of my life. For teaching me the shapes of love, resilience, and the importance of the bonds we share. You are the landscape from which my stories are born and the refuge to which I always return, no matter the distance.

To Chris: My anchor and my steady rhythm. Thank you for holding the blank canvas when I decided to take the leap into this new career as a writer. Your unconditional support has been not only a refuge, but the scaffolding that allowed me to build this dream. Thank you for your patience during my long hours of silence, for the mugs of coffee left gently beside my desk, and for believing in *Canvas of the Hidden Heart* since it was barely a sketch in my mind. You are, and always will be, the red thread that gives meaning to my story.

To everyone who has accompanied me on this journey: thank you for seeing this heart and allowing it to no longer remain hidden.

∞∞∞

About The Author

Hugo Cortés Ruiz

Since childhood, Hugo has been nourished by the wellspring of imagination and deep dreams. Canvas of the Hidden Heart—his second novel—was born from one of those vivid dreams, a story that demanded to be written.

His narrative voice is shaped by personal resilience, having navigated his own difficult seasons of love, the weight of loneliness, and the contrasting warmth of happiness found with others. Now, with a more mature understanding of life's complexities, Hugo has discovered that true love is not always found in grand gestures, but in the quiet details and the kindnesses that people share with him.

Outside of writing, Hugo devotes his time to the people who keep him anchored, believing that the best stories are found in shared silence and honest conversation. He is driven by a desire to explore the fragile beauty of the human heart, crafting narratives that remind us that we are never truly alone in our experiences.

Books By This Author

The Silver Chain: Rebellion In Zacatecas

Deep beneath the arid earth of Zacatecas, silver offers wealth to the empire but binds the people in chains of iron and silence. In a world defined by the brutal hierarchy of the mines, a spark of resistance ignites a fire that threatens to consume the colonial order. From the dust of the rebellion rises a story of sacrifice and unyielding courage. The Silver Chain is a sweeping historical saga that explores the cost of freedom and the strength required to break the bonds of history. A powerful journey through war, heritage, and the enduring fight for human dignity—this is resilience in its rawest form: fierce, tragic, and undeniable.

Valery And The Whispering Teddy Bear

When Valery's brother and sister vanish into their dreams, only her loyal teddy bear, Bubus, knows the truth—they've been taken by the King Ogre of the World of Flowers. Armed with a magical crayon and a brave heart, Valery sets out on an enchanting journey through blooming skies and talking petals to bring them home. Filled with wonder, courage, and the power of love, Valery and the Whispering Teddy Bear is a heartwarming tale about family, forgiveness, and the quiet magic that lives inside every child. Perfect for young readers and dreamers of all ages.

www.ingramcontent.com/pod-product-compliance
Lightning Source LLC
LaVergne TN
LVHW030912080826
845145LV00010B/2861

* 9 7 8 1 0 6 9 6 8 5 1 2 4 *